Vegetarian Cooking

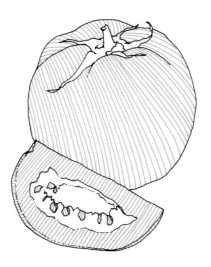

Our Special Thanks

For ideas and inspiration, we extend our appreciation to The Bruised Reed restaurant, Monterey, California, and The Zanzibar restaurant, Santa Cruz, California. For help with cooking and nutritional calculation, thank you, Joyce Lehr. For nutritional advice, our thanks go to Dr. Helene Swenerton, University of California at Davis. And for their cooperation in sharing props for the photographs, thanks go to Agapanthus, Animal Crackers, Color Tile Supermart, House of Today, Murata's, Palo Alto Boots and Hats, Pier 1 Imports, Studio D, Taylor & Ng, The Cupola, TLC, and Williams-Sonoma Kitchenware.

World Publications Group
455 Somerset Avenue
North Dighton, MA 07264

ISBN 1-57215-308-3

Editor: Janeth Johnson Nix
Assistant Editor: Anne K. Turley
Cover design: Lynne Yeamans
Design: Cynthia Bassett
Photography: Tom Wyatt with Evelyn Newell
Illustrations: Kathy Parkinson

Printed and bound in China by Leefung-Asco Printers Ltd.
1 2 3 4 5   06 05 04 03 02

Contents

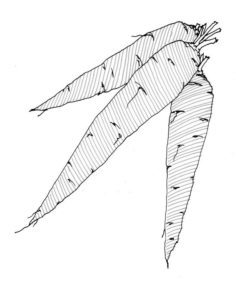

Going Vegetarian

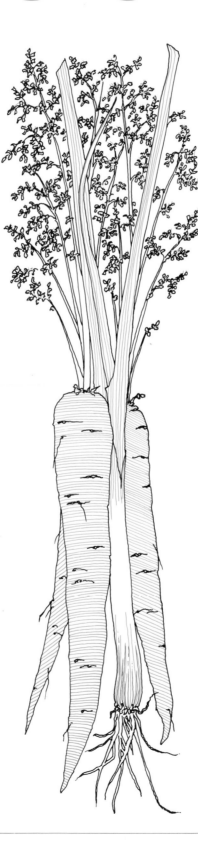

We've heard many reasons for going vegetarian. Some people are just looking for a change of pace from meat and potatoes. Some want to save money. Some want the health advantages of a low-cholesterol, high-fiber diet. Others have religious or philosophical reasons for not eating meat. And there are also those who want to do something about the global food problem.

But whether you want to save money, save your heart, save animals, or save the world from food shortage, you'll need good recipes that sustain your interest in going vegetarian.

And good recipes are the heart of this vegetarian cook book.

We've selected contrasting tastes, colors, and textures and created recipes and menus for dishes that appeal to both eye and appetite. You'll find recipes drawn from the world's great cuisines: Italian pasta dishes, Indian curry dishes, French egg and cheese dishes, and Oriental and Middle Eastern vegetable entrées that will be revelations to your taste buds.

We issue our recipes as irresistible invitations to those who rarely have a meatless meal, as well to those who already know that vegetarian fare is neither fad food nor bland and boring. There are recipes for strict vegetarians who eat neither eggs nor dairy products, and recipes for the ovo-lacto vegetarians, who include eggs and dairy products in their diets.

We think the greatest number of our readers are those who consider themselves part-time vegetarians. Part-time vegetarians enjoy a wide variety of foods and are usually on the lookout for meatless recipes that are exciting and thoroughly satisfying. They don't calculate every amino acid molecule. They shop in ordinary grocery stores and devote ordinary amounts of time to meal preparation; but they aim for extraordinary results with a minimum of fuss.

Indeed, extraordinary results with minimum fuss has been the controlling idea throughout this cook book. Ease of preparation and availability of ingredients were main concerns as we selected recipes. You'll see many recipes in each chapter that fall into the "quick and easy" category. Most ingredients can be purchased at your supermarket. Wheat berries (whole grains of wheat) and soybeans are about the only exceptions. Of course, you may prefer shopping for staples in a health food store, and buying stone-ground flours and cold-pressed oils; the choice is always yours.

Looking ahead

A glance through the chapters in this book should convince even the most skeptical carnivore that vegetarian cooking means far more than bowls of gruel with alfalfa sprouts sprinkled on top.

Starting with salads and appetizers, you'll find unusual side-dish salads and magnificent whole-meal salads.

For a balanced meal, you might want to try the Perfect Protein Salad (page 16) or the Bulgur Supper Salad (page 20). They're both good examples of combining necessary nutrients with a minimum of fuss to present fresh, attractive meals.

In the soup chapter, you'll find a full range of recipes—from family fare like hearty Garden Fresh Minestrone (page 33), to soups guaranteed to impress your guests, such as Cheddar Sherry Soup (page 28), or Almond Soup Gratinée (page 25).

Moving to cheese and egg dishes, you'll discover a stunning collection of omelets, soufflés, and quiches, plus such extraordinary creations as Zesty Tomato Fondue (page 45), Fila Cheese Squares (page 43), and Meringue-topped Vegetable Custard (page 43).

The chapter called "Greens, Grains & Other Good Entrées" takes us to the center of vegetarian cooking—recipes built on the nutritional staples of grains, legumes, and green and yellow vegetables. It also takes us on a discovery trip around the world, with ports of call in Greece, Italy, the Middle East, Japan, and Mexico. And if you've never attempted Indian cooking, here's your opportunity. For incentive, check the photograph on page 63 to see how spectacularly colorful an Indian vegetarian meal can be.

Stir-frying and steaming, two excellent methods for cooking all kinds of vegetables, are featured in the vegetable side-dish chapter. Besides instructions in these basic techniques, we've included a collection of combination vegetable dishes, such as Cauliflower with Broccoli Sauce (page 70) and Curried Carrots with Fruit (page 70).

(Continued on page 8)

 Just a Few Questions, Please...

Won't I get tired of eating nothing but vegetables?
Of course. Anyone would grow tired of eating just spinach and broccoli, but vegetarian cooking includes much more than vegetables. Vegetarian menus include plentiful amounts of legumes and grains, in addition to green and yellow vegetables, and fruit. Many vegetarians also eat eggs and dairy products.

What do you mean by "legumes and grains"?
Legumes are dried beans and peas, including split peas, lentils, soybeans, and a wide variety of red, white, and black beans. Grains are the seeds of cereal plants—wheat, corn, oats, rice, millet, barley, rye. (No, you don't eat them whole, though whole wheat grains, called wheat berries, are delicious.) Most whole grains are milled and made into a variety of different foods —bread, pasta, crêpes, and tortillas, to name a few. Eaten together, legumes and grains are the main source of protein for vegetarians who don't eat eggs and dairy products.

Won't I get fat by eating all those carbohydrates?
Carbohydrates, by themselves, probably won't cause you to gain weight. Eating more calories than you burn is what really pushes up the pounds. Naturally, if you eat too much of a good thing—even whole grain bread—you'll get fat. But before you cut out nutrient-rich whole grains, cut down on excess sugar and fat to lower the number of calories you consume.

Don't I need meat for protein?
No. By weight, soybeans and cheese are better sources of protein than meat and fish. In terms of protein quality, eggs and milk rank above meat. By combining grains and legumes, you can create a protein of higher quality than meat or fish.

Is it true that a meatless diet is good for my health?
That depends. If your doctor has told you to cut down on cholesterol and saturated fats, one way to do it is to cut back on meat; cholesterol appears only in animal products, not in plants. Eggs and whole milk products are also high in cholesterol, so cut back on them, too.

Should I go "cold turkey" on cold turkey, roast beef, and my favorite meats and fish?
We recommend a gradual approach to going vegetarian. For instance, you might want to cut back just on the quantity of meat you serve per meal, or serve meatless meals one, two, or three days a week.

In the beginning, most people who go vegetarian rely on quiches, omelets, cheese pizzas, and the more familiar bean dishes. Gradually, though, they try more adventuresome entrées and international vegetarian dishes.

What makes a meal memorable? Good friends and good conversation, artful presentation of even the simplest dish, and exciting contrasts of texture, taste, and color.

You're on your own for the friends and conversation, but on these two pages we have lots of suggestions for the food. You'll find an international selection of menus, from Mexico to the Orient, plus appealing nonethnic menus. Most are for vegetarians who eat eggs and dairy products. Strict vegetarians will be interested in the Oriental Dinner and the Three-course Vegan Special.

Brunch with Ease

The luscious casserole here can be composed in a jiffy or made ahead, and the bread and dessert are definitely make-ahead items. So on the day you serve this brunch, the only dish you'll have to prepare is Tomatoes Provençal. The ricotta dessert is a do-it-yourself affair that your guests will especially enjoy.

Creamy Spinach-Artichoke Casserole (page 61)
Pebble-top Oatmeal Bread (page 73)
Tomatoes Provençal (page 70)
Brandied Ricotta with Fruit (page 91)

Quiche-Plus for Lunch or Supper

All the "plus" items on this menu are make-ahead dishes. The salad and dessert need to be made ahead—the salad has to marinate and the dessert must be chilled for at least 2 hours. The soup and bread can be made a day in advance, if you like; we suggest treating them as a first course. You might bring the Wheat Berry Batter Bread to the table on a small bread board and slice it there—a nourishing beginning for a cool-weather meal. Then serve the salad alongside the golden wedges of quiche.

Double Mushroom Soup (page 27)
Wheat Berry Batter Bread (page 73)
Golden Cauliflower Quiche (page 41)
Tarragon Vegetable Salad (page 17)
Lemon Yogurt Sponge Torte (page 90)

Lunch or Supper for Summer's End

Family-pleasing menus are always welcome. This one is perfect for late summer or early fall. It contrasts the wonderful seasonal flavors of fresh corn, pears, grapes, and peaches.

Tomato Corn Chowder (page 29)
Casserole Cheese Bread (page 77)
Pear & Grape Slaw (page 17)
Honey Peach Cobbler (page 91)

Dinner from the Middle East

The seasonings are mild but intriguing in this composition of dishes. You can start off with the soup and bread or with the stuffed chard and carrots, whichever you prefer. A simple green salad is optional.

Lemony Lentil Soup (page 30)
Butter-topped Whole Wheat Bread (page 73)
Stuffed Chard or Grape Leaves (page 59)
Steamed Carrots and Crookneck Squash with Savory Cheese Sauce (page 69)
Tossed Green Salad
Yogurt Cheesecake with Dates (page 89)

Winter Picnic

Here's hearty food to warm you during a cold day's outing. You can pack the kettle of hot chili beans in an insulated chest or wrap newspapers and a blanket around it to keep it warm. The hot chocolate can be carried in a thermos, and the tortillas can be wrapped in foil and heated over a grill or camp stove. If the day is too gloomy, you can always heat everything at home and picnic in front of the fireplace.

Layered Chili (page 49)
Whole Wheat Tortillas (page 81)
Hot Chocolate
Juicy Apples
Chewy Bran Bars (page 94)

Three-course Vegan Special

A "vegan" is a strict vegetarian who avoids not only meat, but eggs and dairy products as well. We've designed this menu especially for vegans; though the recipe for soybean soup calls for a little milk, vegetable stock can be used just as well. The soup makes a protein-packed first course, followed by a three-part main course.

Soybean Soup, Bistro-style (page 30)
Cracked Wheat Pilaf
Curried Carrots with Fruit (page 70)
Steamed Broccoli or Green Beans (page 69)
Honey Crunch Baked Apples (page 91) or
Orange Slices with Shredded Coconut

Company Dinner

You'll have to invest some culinary effort in this menu, but the results are impressive. Here's a short cut you can take with the cannelloni: fry the eggplant slices a day ahead, then cover and refrigerate them until you're ready to fill and bake them. You may want to omit the egg garnish from the salad, since it's quite substantial without the egg. Or if red bell peppers are out of season, you can substitute a mixed green salad for the colorful first course.

Roasted Pepper & Tomato Salad (page 14)
Bread Sticks
Eggplant Cannelloni (page 54)
Rice or Risotto
Steamed Italian Green Beans or Swiss Chard
(page 69)
Marzipan Torte (page 89)

Italian Dinner

This family dinner can be served in three or four courses, depending on when you serve the salad. Some people prefer salad before or after the lasagne dish; others like it alongside the hearty entrée.

For a more elaborate meal, you can make the first-course caponata part of a large antipasto platter composed of cheeses, bread sticks, fresh and pickled vegetables, olives, and whatever else Italian strikes your fancy.

Caponata (page 13)
Lasagne Swirls (page 53) or Vegetable Lasagne
(page 53)
Simple Green Salad
Garlic Bread
Sherried Cream with Fruit (page 92)

Mexican Dinner

A good warm-weather menu, this mildly spiced Mexican dinner starts and ends with cooling dishes—a gazpacho for starters and a refreshing fruit with sherbet for dessert. You can buy refried beans, or make your own "refritos" by mashing cooked pinto beans and cooking them with salad oil, butter, or margarine. You can fry your own strips of tortillas, too, or buy tortilla chips.

Make-ahead Gazpacho (page 35)
Chiles Rellenos Casserole (page 51)
Refried Beans
Fried Tortilla Chips (page 32)
Lettuce, Onion & Orange Salad
Cantaloupe Melba (page 93)

Oriental Dinner

This menu allows you to prepare the piquant soybeans and the rice ahead of time. Have the asparagus washed and cut before you serve the soup. When everyone's through with the soup, you stir-fry the asparagus (it takes only a couple of minutes), then serve the soybeans, rice, and asparagus together.

Strict vegetarians may want to substitute a fruit dessert for the Sesame Poundcake, which contains eggs.

Hot & Sour Soup (page 29)
Sweet & Sour Soybeans (page 51)
Brown Rice
Stir-fried Asparagus or Broccoli (page 68)
Sesame Poundcake (page 88)

The breads chapter will make you hungry for a freshly baked slice of Maple-Molasses Bread (page 76) or a herculean sandwich built on your own Honey-Wheat Buns (page 75). Besides quick breads and yeast breads—all chock-full of wholesome whole grains—there are four special pages full of breakfast ideas. Included are recipes for waffles, pancakes, and quick breakfast beverages, plus some revolutionary breakfast ideas, such as Apricot-Almond Sandwiches (page 83) and Peanut Honey Crisps (page 82).

Ready for dessert? A dish of Honey Peach Cobbler (page 91) served hot with vanilla ice cream, perhaps? Or maybe we could tempt you with Ricotta Cheesecake (page 89), a super-rich Marzipan Torte (page 89), or a cooling scoop of Fresh Berry Ice (page 92) and a sliver of Sesame Poundcake (page 88).

Vegetarian cooking bland and boring? We rest our case.

Special features

Every recipe in this cookbook has a special feature—namely, a list of the grams of protein, grams of carbohydrate, milligrams of cholesterol, and number of calories per serving. We offer the information as a resource for those on various diets, or for those simply interested in the approximate nutritional breakdown of recipes.

The numbers were computed with data based on the United States Department of Agriculture's Handbook No. 456. Where a choice of ingredients is given— for instance, most recipes call for butter *or* margarine—the calculations were based on the first item. Of course, if you use margarine instead of butter, the amount of cholesterol per serving will be lower than the amount listed.

Other special features are scattered throughout the book. You'll find out how to make cheese and yogurt (pages 46 and 47), and how

to cope with meat eaters in your family (page 65). For menu suggestions, turn to pages 6 and 7.

Nutrition— knowing what counts

Ours is an age fascinated by analysis and calculation. Even in the kitchen, people are counting like crazy: counting calories, counting cholesterol, counting carbohydrate. And vegetarians—whether full-time or part-time—have to count protein amino acids, right?

Well, not really. Vegetarian cooking doesn't require burdensome homework or recondite information. After all, people have been eating meatless meals for centuries. It's not a strange, exotic way of cooking, nor is it a gimmick diet.

Most vegetarians we know take a moderate approach to counting nutrients. Many of them do little or no nutritional calculation. When we asked vegetarians if they calculate protein intake, a typical response was, "We started out tallying protein grams, but relaxed once we caught on to the idea of protein complementing and realized how easy it was. In a very short time, it just came naturally."

Every vegetarian we've talked and cooked with heartily agrees that all the nutritional calculating in the world won't add up to a hill of soybeans if you and your family don't like what you're cooking. "It's good for you; it's got 10 grams of protein" is no argument if, as the kids say, it tastes yucky. That's why this book features good-tasting, good-looking recipes rather than large doses of nutritional information.

Your grandmother was right

The old-fashioned nutritional advice your grandmother gave still holds: namely, eat a varied, bal-

anced diet. That's the key to menu planning and good general nutrition whether you eat meat or not. In our society, if you eat a variety of foods in a balanced diet, it's extremely unlikely that you're eating too little protein, or too little of almost any nutrient.

A balanced, varied diet of vegetarian foods includes grains (breads, cereals, pasta), legumes (dried beans, peas), vegetables (especially the dark green leafy ones), fruits, dairy products, and eggs.

Each of these food families contributes to a balance of important nutrients: protein, carbohydrate, fats, vitamins, and minerals. Strict vegetarians shun not only meat but also dairy products and eggs. They eat leafy green vegetables for calcium and combine grains, legumes, and vegetables for protein; and many take vitamin supplements for "insurance."

Here's a brief review of important nutrients and nutritional considerations in vegetarian cooking.

Carbohydrate. Carbohydrate is one of the two main sources of energy for physical activity (the other is fat). If we don't eat enough carbohydrate, our versatile body machinery draws eventually on its protein, possibly taking it away from tissue-building and other vital tasks. Grains, legumes, vegetables, and fruits provide carbohydrate in the form of starches and sugars.

"Won't all those caloric starches and sugars make me fat?" That's the most common question asked about the plentiful carbohydrates in a vegetarian diet. The simple answer is no. Consuming more calories than you use makes you fat. Of itself, neither carbohydrate nor any other class of nutrients will add pounds to most people.

If calories are a concern, the best approach is to make every calorie count nutritionally. When you're planning menus, choose sources of carbohydrate that are high in nutrients. This means limiting sweets, sweeteners, and alcohol—they have little to offer other than calories. Instead, concentrate on fruits, vegetables, and other foods that are packed with vitamins and minerals. In a vegetarian diet, beans and grains are important sources of protein as well as carbohydrates.

Beans, rice, breads, pasta, and potatoes aren't by themselves terribly caloric. But beans baked with salt pork and brown sugar, rice dripping with butter, bread slathered with jam, pasta loaded with butter and cheese, and potatoes weighed down with sour cream—there are your excess calories.

Fats. Fats are fattening, aren't they? Indeed, they can be. Fats have more calories per ounce than any other kind of food, but you'd be in trouble if you tried to eliminate them entirely: the fat-soluble vitamins—A, D, K, and E—could not perform their roles, and you'd lack an essential nutrient called linoleic acid.

Fats from animal sources tend to be solid and saturated. Cholesterol, a fatlike substance, is found only in animal fats and animal tissue. If you're turning to meatless menus to cut down on saturated fat and cholesterol, you'll also want to cut down on butter, cheese, whole milk, and eggs (one of the highest sources of cholesterol).

Fats from plant sources tend to be liquid and polyunsaturated. The richest sources of linoleic acid are plant-source fats, especially safflower oil, corn oil, cottonseed oil, and soy oil. When recipes in this book call for "salad oil," you can take your choice.

Vitamins & minerals. Because vitamin B-12 and riboflavin can be in short supply in a strict (no eggs, no dairy products) vegetarian diet, vitamin supplements are recommended. Vegetarians who eat dairy products and eggs usually can satisfy their B-12 and riboflavin needs with a couple of glasses of milk a day, or with milk and an egg or ½ cup of cottage cheese a day.

For excellent sources of vitamins, plus calcium and iron, check the chart on this page. The foods

Nutrition-packed Foods

Vitamins & Minerals	Main Sources
A	carrots, butternut squash, Hubbard squash, sweet potato, cantaloupe, dark leafy greens, papaya, broccoli, red bell pepper, apricots
D	fortified milk, egg yolk (also sunlight)
E	unsaturated oils (especially walnut, sunflower, and safflower), almonds, filberts, walnuts, wheat germ, beet greens, spinach, sweet potato
C	papaya, broccoli, red and green bell pepper, Brussels sprouts, kale, citrus juice, cantaloupe, strawberries, oranges, cauliflower
Thiamin (B-1)	brewer's yeast, whole wheat flour, pinto beans, green peas, wheat germ, soybeans, wheat berries, barley, navy beans, spinach
Riboflavin (B-2)	cottage cheese, milk, yogurt, collards, broccoli, mushrooms, Camembert cheese, okra, butternut squash, asparagus
Niacin	tofu, soybeans, cottage cheese, bulgur wheat, collards, navy beans, fresh and dried peas, pinto beans, kidney beans, lentils
B-6	soybeans, kale, spinach, bananas, buckwheat flour, lentils, garbanzos, pinto beans, black-eyed peas, avocado
Folacin	spinach, brewer's yeast, soybeans, garbanzos, kidney beans, limas, oranges, rye flour, sweet potato, whole wheat flour
B-12	cottage cheese, milk, egg, cheese (such as Edam, Camembert, blue, Cheddar, mozzarella), yogurt
Calcium	dairy products, collards, bok choy, kale, mustard greens, broccoli, okra, tofu, soybeans, corn tortillas
Iron	prune juice, black beans, garbanzos, pinto beans, navy beans, limas, soybeans, lentils, spinach, dried peas

listed as the "main sources" aren't the only sources, but they're the foods most worth considering when you're planning meals for maximum nutrition.

Protein. From the tips of your toenails to the hair on your head, you're protein. Protein means "holding first place" and it is, literally, what holds you together. It's an essential part of your muscles, skin, connective tissue, enzymes, hormones—not to mention hair and nails. The protein you eat keeps all your complex systems in good repair, and it's crucial for children's growth.

The U.S. Recommended Daily Allowance for protein is 46 grams for adult women and 54 grams for men. (Just for comparison, a cup of creamed cottage cheese has 18.6 grams protein; one large egg has 6.5 grams; and 1 cup cooked soybeans has 20 grams.)

Protein from an animal source, especially milk and eggs, contains essential amino acids (those our bodies can't produce themselves) in the proportions our bodies need. That's why animal-source proteins are called complete proteins.

Protein from plant sources, though, with one major exception, has an incomplete amount of one or more essential amino acids. The

exception is soybeans, which provide virtually complete protein. The amino acid present in a limited amount is called the *limiting amino acid* because it limits the usability of the whole protein. For example, if one essential amino acid is 75 percent complete, only 75 percent of the protein can be utilized.

By combining a food that's low in one or two amino acids with a food that's complete in those amino acids, you'll create a high-quality protein combination comparable to animal-source protein. This is called *protein complementing.* Any animal-source protein will complete an incomplete plant protein. Or you can combine two plant-source proteins.

Combining plant sources to make a high-quality, complete protein is part of the kitchen wisdom of most traditional cultures—tortillas and beans, rice and beans, lentil soup and wheat bread, tofu and rice. Even the American kitchen, in its short history, has produced some classic variations on the theme of complementary proteins: macaroni and cheese, a peanut butter sandwich with a glass of milk; beans with cornbread.

Mixing & matching protein

The chart on this page combines the traditional knowledge of food families with the modern contribution of amino acid analysis. By combining foods from different columns, you'll be able to create varieties of high-quality protein.

The chart lists sources of protein according to their limiting amino acids. The first column includes foods that have virtually no limiting

What's missing? There are so many beautiful good foods to serve vegetarian-style, it's easy to forget about meat.

amino acid: dairy products, eggs, and soybeans. They can be used as high-quality protein sources by themselves or as a boost to any food in any of the other columns.

The other columns each contain foods low in a certain essential amino acid. To make a complete protein, you combine a food from one of these columns with a different food from one of the others.

You'll notice that families of plant foods tend to be low in the same amino acids. Looking down the columns, you see the two main plant families for protein: grains and legumes. The strengths of grains make up for the weaknesses of legumes, and vice versa. To take you a long way toward meeting your daily protein needs, combine a grain food from the second column with a legume from the third or fourth column.

The vegetables, nuts, and seeds also contribute protein to your diet, though their contribution is less than that from grains and legumes.

Mix & Match for Complete Protein

Combine Different Foods From Any Two Columns

No Limiting Amino Acid	Low in Lysine	Low in Sulfur-carrying Amino Acids	Low in Tryptophan

Dairy products
  Cheese (except cream cheese)
  Cottage cheese
  Milk, all types, including powdered
  Yogurt
Eggs
  Whole, and egg whites
Legumes
  Soybeans
  Soybean curd (tofu)
  Soy milk
	Legumes
	  Peanuts
	Grains
	  Barley
	  Buckwheat
	  Bulgur wheat
	  Cornmeal
	  Millet
	  Oats
	  Rice
	  Rye
	  Wheat
	Nuts & Seeds
	  Almonds
	  Brazil nuts
	  *Cashews
	  Coconut
	  Filberts
	  Pecans
	  Pumpkin seeds
	  Sunflower seeds
	  Walnuts
	Vegetables
	  Asparagus
	  Beet greens
	  Corn
	  Kale
	  Mushrooms
	  *Potato
	  Sweet potato
	  Yams
		Legumes
		  Beans, dried (black, pinto, red, white)
		  Black-eyed peas, dried
		  Garbanzos
		  Lentils
		  Limas
		  Mung beans
		  *Peanuts
		Nuts
		  Filberts
		Vegetables
		  Asparagus
		  Beans, green
		  Beet greens
		  Broccoli
		  Brussels sprouts
		  Mushrooms
		  Parsley
		  Peas, green
		  Potatoes
		  Soybeans
		  Swiss chard
			Legumes
			  *Beans, dried (black, pinto, red, white)
			  Garbanzos
			  Limas
			  Mung beans
			  *Peanuts
			Grains
			  Cornmeal
			Nuts
			  Almonds
			  Brazil nuts
			  *Walnuts, English
			Vegetables
			  Corn
			  Beet greens
			  Mushrooms
			  Peas, green
			  *Swiss chard

*Indicates foods containing more than 90 percent of ideal amount.

Salads & Appetizers

Delicate, ruffled lettuce leaves, bold-colored beets and carrots, glorious red peppers, creamy-white mushrooms, fruits of all varieties—there's really nothing in a farmers' market of produce that can't go into a salad or appetizer.

In the face of such a wealth of possibilities, our selection of recipes for this chapter was particularly difficult. We narrowed our testing to foods with a certain spunky character that we felt would go well with other vegetarian fare.

When you start improvising on your own—and many of the best salads and appetizers are improvised from fresh ingredients you just happen to have on hand—you'll want to follow the same guidelines we use in testing. First of all, use the freshest possible ingredients. Then, think in terms of contrasts and select a variety of shapes, colors, tastes, and textures. Finally, present your salads and appetizers in the most beautiful and appealing way possible.

The first four recipes in this chapter are appetizers. You'll find an elegant Mushroom Almond Pâté (page 13), a lively Italian eggplant Caponata (page 13), a three-layered Vegetable Terrine (page 13), and Hummus (page 14).

After the appetizer recipes comes a banquet of side-dish and whole-meal salads. Some use spring and summertime ingredients, others include winter vegetables, still others are made of produce that's available all year.

For a simple supper, you might want to tease the palate with Mushroom, Blue Cheese & Walnut Salad (page 14) before serving a plain omelet. Or maybe you'll choose to do all the work a day ahead and prepare a magnificent platter of cooked marinated vegetables, called Vegetables à la Grecque (page 16). You can follow the vegetables with delicious Baked Brie (page 45).

In contrast to our side-dish salads that provide mainly vitamins, minerals, and fiber, our whole-meal salads generally live up to their name and provide a balanced whole meal to serve with bread or rolls.

But what about serving just a plain tossed green salad? Fine! More power to the greens! Freshness is the key in all salads and is especially appreciated when just one or two types of lettuce or other greens are used. In general, the more delicate the ingredients, the more delicate the dressing should be. At the end of the chapter, you'll find two dressings for mixed greens, and a low-calorie dressing that's delightful on fresh fruit.

Mushroom Almond Pâté

For occasions that call for an elegant appetizer, try this well-seasoned pâté. Serve it from a crock with crackers for an hors d'oeuvre. As a first course, it can be sliced and presented on plates along with crusty bread and tiny sweet gherkins, if you wish.

> 1 cup slivered almonds
> ¼ cup butter or margarine
> 1 small onion, chopped
> 1 clove garlic, minced or pressed
> ¾ pound mushrooms, sliced
> ¾ teaspoon salt
> ½ teaspoon thyme leaves
> ⅛ teaspoon white pepper
> 2 tablespoons salad oil

Spread almonds in a shallow pan and toast in a 350° oven for about 8 minutes or until lightly browned.

Melt butter in a wide frying pan over medium-high heat. Add onion, garlic, mushrooms, salt, thyme, and pepper. Cook, stirring occasionally, until onion is soft and most of pan juices have evaporated.

In a food processor or blender, whirl almonds to form a paste. With motor running, add oil and whirl until creamy. Add mushroom mixture and whirl until pâté is smooth. Makes eight ¼-cup servings.

Per serving: 4 grams protein, 6 grams carbohydrate, 35 milligrams cholesterol, 234 calories.

Vegetable Terrine

Here's a superb appetizer—exclusively yours from Ma Maison, a Los Angeles restaurant so celebrated it has an unlisted phone number. You make a combination of carrots and mushrooms for the bottom and top layers, and use a spinach mixture for the center layer. Eggs and Swiss cheese bind the colorful vegetables and make it easy to slice.

> 8 tablespoons (¼ lb.) butter
> 8 medium-size (2 lbs.) carrots, cut in ½-inch slices
> ½ pound mushrooms, sliced
> 1 package (10 oz.) frozen chopped spinach, thawed
> 5 eggs
> 1 cup (4 oz.) shredded Swiss cheese
> 1 teaspoon salt
> ½ teaspoon pepper
> ⅛ teaspoon ground nutmeg

Melt 4 tablespoons of the butter in a wide frying pan over medium-high heat. Add carrots and cook, stirring, for 2 minutes. Reduce heat to low; cover and simmer carrots until tender (about 15 minutes). Coarsely chop carrots and set aside in a large mixing bowl.

In the same pan, cook mushrooms in 2 more tablespoons of the butter until mushrooms are limp and all liquid has evaporated. Coarsely chop mushrooms and add to carrots. Let cool.

Squeeze as much liquid as possible from spinach. In same pan, cook spinach in the remaining 2 tablespoons butter for 2 minutes. Let cool.

In a bowl, beat together 4 of the eggs. Add cheese, salt, pepper, and nutmeg; mix well. Stir into cooled carrot-mushroom mixture. Beat remaining egg lightly, then combine with spinach. Fold lengthwise into thirds a 15-inch length of foil. Line bottom and both ends of a 9 by 5-inch loaf pan with foil. Generously butter foil and pan sides. Spread half the carrot mixture in pan. Cover with spinach mixture. Spread remaining carrot mixture over top.

Cover pan tightly with foil and set in a larger pan containing at least 1 inch of scalding water. Bake in a 400° oven until a knife inserted in center comes out clean (about 1 hour and 15 minutes). Remove from oven and let stand for 10 minutes. Run a knife around sides of pan. Invert onto a serving platter and carefully lift off foil. Cut in slices and serve warm or at room temperature. Makes 8 servings.

Per serving: 11 grams protein, 14 grams carbohydrate, 207 milligrams cholesterol, 269 calories.

Caponata

Enjoy an Italian-style first course—spoon this piquant eggplant mixture onto crisp lettuce and pass around crusty bread. Caponata would also be good as part of an antipasto selection.

> 2 cups diced celery
> ½ cup olive oil
> 1 medium-size unpeeled eggplant, cut in ¾-inch cubes
> 1 large onion, chopped
> ⅓ cup wine vinegar
> 1 teaspoon sugar
> 2 large tomatoes, peeled and diced
> 1 cup water
> 1 tablespoon capers
> ¼ cup sliced pimento-stuffed olives
> 1 can (about 2¼ oz.) sliced ripe olives, drained
> 2 tablespoons minced parsley
> Salt (optional)

In a wide frying pan over medium heat, cook celery in oil, stirring occasionally, until soft. Remove with a slotted spoon and set aside.

Add eggplant to pan and cook, stirring, until it is lightly browned and tender enough to mash easily. Add onion and continue cooking until onion is soft. Remove eggplant and onion with a slotted spoon and add to celery.

Add to pan the vinegar, sugar, tomatoes, and water; cook, stirring occasionally, for 5 minutes.

Return vegetables to pan. Stir in capers, olives, and parsley. Reduce heat and simmer, uncovered, until most of liquid evaporates (about 20 minutes). Add salt to taste, if desired. Cool, cover, and chill until next day or for as long as 1 week. Bring to room temperature before serving. Makes 8 servings.

Per serving: 2 grams protein, 8 grams carbohydrate, no cholesterol, 166 calories.

Hummus

(Pictured on page 58)

For a classic presentation of this Middle Eastern dish, spread hummus on a rimmed plate. Make a design with a spatula, then drizzle olive oil over it. Or simply garnish hummus with parsley. Pocket bread makes a fine accompaniment.

> **1 can (15 oz.) garbanzos**
> **¼ cup tahine (sesame paste), or ¼ cup toasted sesame seeds and 2 tablespoons olive oil**
> **3 tablespoons lemon juice**
> **1 large clove garlic, cut in thirds**
> **¼ teaspoon ground cumin**
> **Salt and pepper**
> **Optional garnishes: Olive oil or chopped parsley**

Drain garbanzos, reserving liquid. Put garbanzos into a blender or food processor. Add tahine (or toasted sesame seeds and olive oil), lemon juice, garlic, cumin, and ¼ cup of the garbanzo liquid. Whirl, adding more garbanzo liquid if needed, until mixture is smooth and the consistency of heavy batter. Season to taste with salt and pepper. Garnish as suggested above. Makes 12 servings, 2 tablespoons per serving.

Per serving: 4 grams protein, 11 grams carbohydrate, no cholesterol, 97 calories.

Mushroom, Blue Cheese & Walnut Salad

Marinated fresh mushrooms, zesty blue cheese, and crunchy walnuts make a lively first-course salad. For a meal that is well balanced, both nutritionally and esthetically, follow the salad with a simple omelet.

> **¼ cup olive oil or salad oil**
> **2 teaspoons dry basil leaves**
> **½ teaspoon salt**
> **⅛ teaspoon *each* pepper and paprika**
> **2 teaspoons Dijon mustard**
> **5 teaspoons white wine vinegar**
> **½ pound mushrooms, sliced**
> **2 green onions (including tops), thinly sliced**
> **⅔ cup broken walnut pieces**
> **4 ounces blue-veined cheese, coarsely crumbled**
> **4 cups bite-size pieces of romaine or butter lettuce leaves**
> **About 10 cherry tomatoes, whole or halved**

In a salad bowl, combine oil, basil, salt, pepper, paprika, mustard, and vinegar. Beat with a fork until blended. Mix in mushrooms and green onions; let stand at room temperature to marinate for at least 30 minutes.

Add walnut pieces, blue cheese, lettuce, and cherry tomatoes and toss lightly. Makes 4 servings.

Per serving: 12 grams protein, 12 grams carbohydrate, 25 milligrams cholesterol, 407 calories.

Roasted Pepper & Tomato Salad

(Pictured on facing page)

Late summer is the time to enjoy this Mediterranean-inspired roasted pepper salad. If you've never tried a roasted pepper, you're likely to be pleasantly intrigued by its nutty, mellow flavor and tender-crisp texture.

This salad is an excellent appetizer, but it also makes a marvelous full meal accompanied by a cheese board, iced tea or wine, and crusty bread.

> **6 large red or green bell peppers or a combination of both**
> **5 large tomatoes (about 2½ lbs.)**
> **20 pitted ripe olives**
> **¼ cup olive oil**
> **½ teaspoon salt**
> **¼ teaspoon pepper**
> **1 teaspoon ground cumin**
> **4 cloves garlic, minced or pressed**
> **1 tablespoon chopped parsley**
> **Lettuce leaves**
> **6 hard-cooked eggs**

Set whole peppers in a shallow pan and place in broiler so that peppers are about 1 inch from heat source. Broil, turning frequently with tongs, until peppers are well blistered and charred on all sides. Then place in a paper bag, close bag tightly, and let peppers sweat for 15 to 20 minutes to loosen skins. Cool and strip off skins. Cut peppers in half and remove and discard stems and seeds. Cut peppers into strips roughly ½ by 1 inch and place in a bowl.

Peel tomatoes and cut in half; remove and discard seeds. Cut into bite-size pieces and add to peppers along with olives.

In another bowl, combine oil, salt, pepper, cumin, garlic, and parsley; stir well to blend. Stir into

(Continued on page 16)

Red peppers are hot, right? Not when they're mellow red bell peppers roasted to bring out their nutlike flavor. Enjoy them in Roasted Pepper & Tomato Salad (recipe on this page), accompanied by assorted cheeses and French bread.

pepper mixture; taste and add more salt and pepper, if desired.

Cover salad and let stand at room temperature for about 4 hours, or refrigerate for as long as two days (but bring to room temperature before serving).

To serve, line individual plates with lettuce leaves and mound pepper mixture onto lettuce. Garnish each salad with eggs, cut in halves or quarters. Makes 6 servings.

Per serving: 10 grams protein, 13 grams carbohydrate, 352 milligrams cholesterol, 245 calories.

Perfect Protein Salad

Here's a beautifully composed salad. It's brimming with delightful textures, colors, and tastes—and it's packed with protein. You can serve it as a main course or side dish.

2 large heads butter lettuce
10 medium-size mushrooms
1 medium-size carrot, sliced
½ cup Spanish-style peanuts
3 tablespoons chopped parsley
2 tablespoons *each* wheat germ, sunflower seeds, and unsweetened granola-type cereal
½ cup *each* bean sprouts and shredded jack cheese
¾ cup plain yogurt
3 tablespoons salad oil
1½ tablespoons lemon juice
Salt and pepper
1 small avocado
2 hard-cooked eggs, quartered

Line a large serving bowl with outer leaves of lettuce. Tear inner leaves into bite-size pieces. Place in bowl and mix with mushrooms, carrot, and peanuts. Sprinkle in parsley, wheat germ, sunflower seeds, cereal, sprouts, and cheese.

In a small bowl, blend yogurt, oil, and lemon juice. Pour dressing over salad; toss gently. Season to taste with salt and pepper. Peel, pit, and slice avocado. Garnish salad with eggs and avocado slices. Makes 6 servings.

Per serving: 12 grams protein, 14 grams carbohydrate, 54 milligrams cholesterol, 315 calories.

Vegetables à la Grecque

The French style of simmering a variety of vegetables in the Greek manner (with herbs, lemon juice, and oil) and marinating them in this same sauce, concentrated, results in a superbly seasoned salad.

The basic recipe suits a wide range of vegetables, and though it takes more time to cook a variety, rather than a single vegetable, that's part of the fun. Cook vegetables that appeal to you, then arrange them handsomely on a platter.

3½ cups water
6 tablespoons lemon juice
¾ cup dry white wine
½ cup olive oil
1½ teaspoons salt
2 bay leaves
2 cloves garlic, cut in thirds
1 shallot or 1 large green onion, chopped
6 whole black peppers
1 teaspoon *each* dry tarragon and thyme leaves
Vegetables (directions follow)
2 tablespoons chopped parsley

In a large Dutch oven or other wide pan, place water, lemon juice,

wine, oil, salt, and bay leaves. In a tea ball or cheesecloth bag, enclose garlic, shallot, peppers, tarragon, and thyme; add to pan. Bring to a boil, then lower heat; cover and simmer for 10 minutes.

Add vegetables and cook according to directions that follow. With a slotted spoon, remove vegetables as they are cooked and place in a shallow pan. When all vegetables are cooked, remove tea ball or cheesecloth bag from pan and discard herbs. Increase heat to medium and cook broth until reduced to one cup; cool slightly, then spoon sauce over vegetables.

Cover and refrigerate for at least 4 hours or as long as 3 days. To serve, lift vegetables from sauce, arrange on a platter, and garnish with parsley. Makes 8 servings.

Per serving (including all vegetables listed below): 4 grams protein, 17 grams carbohydrate, no cholesterol, 211 calories.

Summer squash. Remove ends from 2 small crookneck squash and slice squash in half lengthwise. Remove ends from 3 small zucchini and slice in half lengthwise; cut each half again lengthwise. Add to broth, cover, and simmer until crisp-tender (about 5 minutes).

Carrots. Peel 3 carrots and slice on the diagonal about ½-inch thick. Add to broth; cover and simmer until crisp-tender (about 7 minutes).

Leeks. Cut 3 leeks in half lengthwise, then cut into 4-inch lengths; discard coarse leaves. Wash thoroughly to remove sand. Add to broth; cover and simmer until tender (about 7 minutes).

Eggplant. Cut 1 small (¾ lb.) unpeeled eggplant in half lengthwise, then slice into 1-inch-thick strips. Add to broth; cover and simmer until tender (about 7 minutes).

Mushrooms. Remove ends from ½ pound small mushrooms; wash mushrooms. Add to broth; cover and simmer until barely tender (about 3 minutes).

Bell pepper (red or green). Seed and cut 3 peppers into 1-inch-wide strips. Add to broth; cover and simmer until barely tender (about 5 minutes).

Onions. Trim and peel 8 small boiling onions. Add to broth; cover and simmer until tender (7 to 9 minutes).

Celery hearts. Remove ends from 3 celery hearts and cut off tops to make 4-inch-long pieces; cut each piece in half lengthwise. Add to broth; cover and simmer until tender (about 15 minutes).

Tarragon Vegetable Salad

Take a hint from French cooks and marinate cooked vegetables for a delicious salad. Because the frozen peas and carrots are only thawed, not cooked, they taste and look extraordinarily fresh in this recipe.

½ cup olive oil or salad oil

3 tablespoons white wine vinegar

1 tablespoon chopped parsley

1 teaspoon *each* salt and tarragon leaves

2 teaspoons Dijon mustard

½ teaspoon pepper

1 shallot, finely chopped (or ¼ cup chopped green onion)

1 pound small thin-skinned potatoes

1 pound green beans, cut in 1-inch lengths

1 pound turnips, peeled and cut in ½-inch squares

2 packages (10 oz. *each*) frozen mixed carrots and peas, thawed

Lettuce leaves

About 8 cherry tomatoes

Stir together oil, vinegar, parsley, salt, tarragon, mustard, pepper, and shallot; set aside.

Place potatoes in 1 inch boiling water; cover and cook just until tender when pierced (about 20

minutes); drain. When cool enough to handle, peel and cut into ¼-inch-thick slices.

Meanwhile, steam green beans over boiling water for about 7 minutes or until crisp-tender. Rinse with cold water and drain well. Steam turnips over boiling water for about 8 minutes or until tender when pierced. Rinse with cold water and drain well.

In a large bowl, combine potatoes, beans, turnips, and thawed carrots and peas. Pour dressing over all and stir gently. Cover and chill for at least 8 hours or until next day; stir occasionally.

About 1 hour before serving, line a shallow serving dish with lettuce leaves and halve the cherry tomatoes. Mound salad in center of lettuce and garnish with tomato halves. Let stand at room temperature until serving time. Makes 8 servings.

Per serving: 5 grams protein, 25 grams carbohydrate, no cholesterol, 237 calories.

Turkish Eggplant Salad

You bake an eggplant until it collapses, then mix the pulp with green pepper and yogurt for a calorie-lean salad. You might feature it as a first course, garnished with tomato, onion rings, and romaine spears.

1 large (about 1½ lbs.) eggplant

1 tablespoon *each* olive oil and lemon juice

1 clove garlic, minced or pressed

1 medium-size green pepper, seeded and finely chopped

1 cup plain yogurt

Salt and pepper

Romaine lettuce leaves

3 tomatoes

1 small red onion

2 tablespoons chopped parsley

With a fork, pierce skin of eggplant. Place eggplant in a rimmed pan. Bake in a 400° oven for 1 hour or until very soft. Cool. Split in half and scoop out pulp into a bowl. Mash pulp with a fork. Mix in oil, lemon juice, garlic, green pepper, yogurt, and salt and pepper to taste. Cover and chill for 2 hours.

To serve, arrange romaine leaves on individual salad plates. Mound eggplant in center of each. Cut tomatoes in wedges. Thinly slice onion and separate into rings. Surround salad with tomato wedges and top with onion rings and parsley. Makes 6 servings.

Per serving: 4 grams protein, 13 grams carbohydrate, 3 milligrams cholesterol, 87 calories.

Pear & Grape Slaw

Orange-flavored yogurt enfolds this luscious mixture of grapes, pears, cabbage, celery, and green onions.

4 cups finely shredded cabbage

2 green onions (including tops), thinly sliced

1 stalk celery, thinly sliced

2 cups seedless grapes

¼ cup slivered almonds

1 carton (8 oz.) orange-flavored yogurt

3 firm ripe Bartlett pears

Salt and pepper

2 tablespoons finely chopped crystallized ginger

(Continued on page 19)

...Pear & Grape Slaw (cont'd.)

In a serving bowl, combine cabbage, green onion, celery, and grapes; cover and chill to crisp.

Spread almonds in a shallow pan and toast in a 350° oven for about 8 minutes or until lightly browned.

Just before serving, place yogurt in a bowl. Halve, core, and thinly slice pears into yogurt; stir lightly, making sure each slice is coated to keep pears from darkening. Mix pears and yogurt into the salad and season to taste with salt and pepper. Sprinkle toasted nuts and ginger over top. Makes 8 servings.

Per serving: 3 grams protein, 28 grams carbohydrate, 1 milligram cholesterol, 139 calories.

Salad-in-a-Boat

(Pictured on facing page)

A creamy, crunchy mixture of vegetables and eggs sails forth in a puffy pastry boat—an ingenious way to launch a main-dish salad. You can bake the cheese-flavored pastry boat a day ahead. You can even fill the boat several hours before serving, since the layer of spinach keeps the salad mixture from soaking into the crust.

⅔ **cup water**

5 **tablespoons butter or margarine**

¼ **teaspoon salt**

⅔ **cup all-purpose flour**

3 **eggs**

¾ **cup (3 oz.) shredded Swiss cheese**

1½ **cups small spinach leaves**

Egg-Vegetable Salad (recipe follows)

8 **cherry tomatoes**

Summertime fare with a flair—that's Salad-in-a-Boat (recipe above). It's an attractive, easy-to-make entrée, shown here with Sesame Pound Cake (recipe on page 88) and a cooling blend of equal parts mint tea and orange juice.

In a 2-quart pan, bring water, butter, and salt to a boil. When butter melts, remove pan from heat and add flour all at once. Beat until well blended.

Return pan to medium heat and stir rapidly for 1 minute or until a ball forms in middle of pan and a film forms on bottom of pan. Remove pan from heat and beat in eggs, one at a time, until mixture is smooth and glossy. Add cheese and beat until well mixed. Spoon into a greased 9-inch round pan with removable bottom or spring-release sides. Spread evenly over bottom and up sides of pan.

Bake crust in a 400° oven for 40 minutes or until puffed and brown; turn off oven. With a wooden pick, prick crust in 10 to 12 places; leave in closed oven for about 10 minutes to dry. Remove pan from oven and cool completely. Remove crust from pan.

Prepare egg vegetable salad. Line bottom and sides of boat with spinach leaves. Cut each tomato in half. Pile egg salad over spinach and garnish with cherry tomatoes. Cut boat in thick wedges. Makes 6 servings.

Per serving (including salad): 18 grams protein, 19 grams carbohydrate, 436 milligrams cholesterol, 483 calories.

Egg-Vegetable Salad. In a bowl, stir together ½ cup **mayonnaise,** 1 teaspoon **Dijon mustard,** and ¼ teaspoon ground **cumin.** Stir in 1 cup thinly sliced raw **cauliflower,** ¼ pound raw **mushrooms** (thinly sliced), 1 cup frozen **peas** (thawed), 1 cup thinly sliced **celery,** and 2 **green onions** and tops (thinly sliced). Coarsely chop 6 **hard-cooked eggs;** gently fold into vegetable mixture.

Zucchini Fiesta Salad

Introduce your favorite Mexican entrée with this spring-fresh salad.

Bright green zucchini and pretty yellow crookneck squash mix with distinctive Mexican ingredients—cumin, green chilies, and avocado—for a fiesta of flavors.

½ **pound** *each* **small zucchini and crookneck squash, cut crosswise in ¼-inch-thick slices**

2 **tablespoons lemon juice**

¼ **cup salad oil**

½ **teaspoon salt**

 Dash *each* **of pepper and ground cumin**

1 **green onion (including top), thinly sliced**

⅓ **cup diced green chilies**

⅓ **cup pimento-stuffed olives, cut in half crosswise**

1 **small package (3 oz.) cream cheese, cut in ¾-inch cubes**

1 **small avocado**

 Lettuce leaves

 Fresh coriander (cilantro) sprigs

Steam zucchini and crookneck squash over boiling water until crisp-tender (about 3 minutes). Plunge into ice water to cool; drain well.

In a large bowl, combine lemon juice, oil, salt, pepper, and cumin. Add drained squash and stir lightly; chill for 30 minutes. Add onion, chilies, olives, and cheese. Peel and pit avocado; cut into small cubes. Add to salad and mix lightly.

To serve, arrange lettuce leaves on 4 salad plates. Mound equal portions of salad on each plate. Garnish each salad with a sprig of coriander. Makes 4 servings.

Per serving: 5 grams protein, 10 grams carbohydrate, 24 milligrams cholesterol, 335 calories.

Vegetable-Herb Salad

For a show-off salad that can steal the scene at a party or on a buffet, assemble this salad in a glass serving bowl so each colorful layer can be seen. You can serve it after an hour's chilling or make it a day ahead—it won't wilt.

> 4 cups shredded iceberg lettuce
> ⅔ cup chopped parsley
> 1 green or red bell pepper, seeded and coarsely chopped
> 2 cups coarsely chopped cauliflower or broccoli
> 3 stalks celery, thinly sliced
> 2 *each* large carrots and zucchini, shredded
> 1 package (10 oz.) frozen peas, thawed
> 1 cup *each* mayonnaise and plain yogurt
> 2 tablespoons Dijon mustard
> 1 teaspoon *each* dry rosemary, dry basil, and oregano leaves
> 2 teaspoons garlic salt
> ½ teaspoon pepper
> 2½ cups (10 oz.) shredded Cheddar cheese
> 2 green onions (including tops), thinly sliced
> ⅓ cup sunflower seeds

In a shallow 4-quart serving dish, place lettuce in an even layer. Distribute parsley, green pepper, cauliflower, celery, carrots, zucchini, and peas in even layers over lettuce. Mix mayonnaise, yogurt, mustard, rosemary, basil, oregano, garlic salt, and pepper. Spread evenly over top. Sprinkle cheese and onions over dressing, then sprinkle sunflower seeds over all. Cover and chill up to 24 hours. Makes 12 servings.

Per serving: 10 grams protein, 9 grams carbohydrate, 38 milligrams cholesterol, 288 calories.

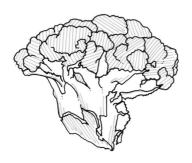

Zucchini & Apple Salad

Fruit and vegetables make a crisp combination that's perfect as a side dish with blintzes, kugel, or any noodle-and-cheese dish. Prepare the salad ahead of time so the flavors have a chance to blend.

> ⅓ cup salad oil
> 1 tablespoon lemon juice
> 2 tablespoons white wine vinegar
> 1 teaspoon *each* sugar and dry basil
> About ¾ teaspoon salt
> ¼ teaspoon pepper
> 3 medium-size red or golden Delicious apples
> ½ medium-size red onion, thinly sliced lengthwise
> 1 green pepper, seeded and cut into matchstick pieces
> 1 pound zucchini, thinly sliced

In a large salad bowl, combine oil, lemon juice, vinegar, sugar, basil, salt, and pepper. Core and dice unpeeled apples and add to dressing; coat apples well with dressing. Add onion, green pepper, and zucchini. Stir lightly. Cover and chill.

Just before serving, mix salad again until well combined. Taste and add more salt if needed. Makes 8 servings.

Per serving: 1 gram protein, 10 grams carbohydrate, no cholesterol, 122 calories.

Tabbuli

It's worth growing a pot of mint just to make this classic fresh-tasting Middle Eastern salad. Traditionally, the bulgur is just soaked in water, but we like to cook it lightly to intensify the wheaty flavor. Be careful not to overcook it, though—the bulgur should still have crunch.

Spinach and Feta Quiche (page 41) would go well with tabbuli, as would Feta Cheese Squares (page 43) or Stuffed Grape Leaves (page 59).

> 1 cup bulgur wheat
> 1 cup water
> ⅓ cup olive oil or salad oil
> ¼ cup lemon juice
> 1 teaspoon *each* salt and ground allspice
> 1 cup chopped green onions (including tops)
> ¼ cup chopped fresh mint leaves
> 1 cup chopped parsley
> ½ cup cooked garbanzo beans
> 2 tomatoes, finely diced
> 1 head romaine lettuce, washed and chilled

Bring bulgur and water to a boil in a covered pan. Immediately reduce heat and simmer covered, for 5 minutes or until liquid is absorbed; bulgur should still be crunchy. Turn bulgur into a bowl and mix in oil, lemon juice, salt, and allspice. Cool.

Add onions, mint, parsley, garbanzos, and tomatoes. Mix together lightly. Cover and chill for 1 hour or until next day.

To serve, line a platter with large outer romaine leaves; pile tabbuli in center. Arrange inner romaine leaves on a separate serving plate. To eat tabbuli, take inner leaf of romaine and use it to scoop up each bite. Makes 6 servings.

Per serving: 11 grams protein, 50 grams carbohydrate, no cholesterol, 363 calories.

Bulgur Supper Salad

The toasty whole-grain flavor of bulgur—quick-cooking cracked wheat—goes well with all kinds of vegetables. Here it's tossed with a spicy mustard dressing and mixed with artichoke hearts, carrots, celery, green pepper, and onions for a splendid whole-meal salad.

- 2 **cups water**
- ¾ **teaspoon salt**
- 1 **vegetable-flavored bouillon cube**
- 1 **cup bulgur wheat**
  Mustard Dressing (recipe follows)
- 1 **jar (6 oz.) marinated artichoke hearts**
- 1 **large carrot, shredded**
- 2 **stalks celery, thinly sliced**
- 1 **green pepper, seeded and diced**
- 2 **green onions (including tops), thinly sliced**
- ½ **cup chopped parsley**
  About 8 lettuce leaves
- 3 **hard-cooked eggs, quartered**
- 2 **medium-size tomatoes, cut in wedges**
- 4 **ounces sharp Cheddar or Swiss cheese, cut into julienne strips**
  About ¼ cup pitted ripe olives

In a 3-quart pan, bring water, salt, and vegetable bouillon cube to boiling. Stir in bulgur. Reduce heat; cover and simmer for 15 minutes.

Meanwhile prepare Mustard Dressing. Drain marinade from artichokes into dressing, mixing it well. Dice artichokes and set aside.

Turn hot cooked bulgur into a bowl, add dressing, and stir gently. Let stand until cool. Stir in artichokes, carrot, celery, green pepper, onions, and parsley. Cover and refrigerate for 2 hours or until next day.

Arrange lettuce on a serving platter or individual plates. Mound salad on lettuce; surround with eggs and tomatoes. Sprinkle cheese over top and garnish with olives. Makes 8 servings.

Per serving (including dressing): 10 grams protein, 26 grams carbohydrate, 108 milligrams cholesterol, 682 calories.

Mustard Dressing. In a bowl, combine 4 tablespoons *each* **salad oil** and **lemon juice**, 1 teaspoon *each* dry **basil** and **oregano** leaves, ½ teaspoon **pepper**, 1 clove **garlic** (minced or pressed), and 1 tablespoon **Dijon mustard**.

Russian Potato Salad

Potato salad is pale, soft, and bland, right? Wrong. Not when it's Russian! Then it's colorful, crisp, and tangy because it's full of apples, carrots, pickled beets, red onion, green pepper—and, of course, potatoes.

- 1 **pound thin-skinned potatoes**
  Caper Dressing (recipe follows)
- 2 **medium-size apples, unpeeled**
- 3 **medium size carrots, thinly sliced**
- 1 **small red onion, chopped**
- 1 **medium-size green pepper, seeded and cut into strips**
- 1 **can (1 lb.) pickled beets, drained and diced**

Place potatoes in 1-inch boiling water; cover and cook just until tender when pierced (20 to 25 minutes).

Meanwhile, prepare dressing in a large bowl. Drain potatoes, cool, peel, and dice directly into dressing. Also dice apples into dressing (to prevent browning). Add carrots, onion, green pepper, and beets. Stir lightly. Cover and refrigerate for 6 hours or until next day. Makes 10 servings.

Per serving (including dressing): 2 grams protein, 18 grams carbohydrate, no cholesterol, 173 calories.

Caper Dressing. Stir together 3 tablespoons *each* **white wine vinegar** and **capers**, ½ cup **salad oil**, 2 teaspoons **sugar**, 1 teaspoon *each* **dry mustard** and **salt**, ½ teaspoon **dill weed**, and ¼ teaspoon *each* **pepper** and **paprika**.

Quick Artichoke Pasta Salad

(Pictured on page 23)

The liquid from marinated artichoke hearts turns into a zingy dressing for this marvelously simple macaroni salad. It's delicious served with a frittata or Vegetarian Joe (page 44), or with a minestrone soup.

- 4 **ounces (about 1 cup) salad macaroni or other medium-size pasta**
- 1 **jar (6 oz.) marinated artichoke hearts**
- ¼ **pound mushrooms, quartered**
- 1 **cup cherry tomatoes, halved**
- 1 **cup medium-size pitted ripe olives**
- 1 **tablespoon chopped parsley**
- ½ **teaspoon dry basil leaves**
  Salt and pepper

Cook macaroni according to package directions; drain well, rinse with cold water, and drain again. Turn into a large bowl.

Add artichokes and their liquid, mushrooms, cherry tomatoes, olives, parsley, and basil; toss gently. Cover and refrigerate for at least 4 hours or until next day. Before serving, season with salt and pepper to taste. Makes 6 servings.

Per serving: 5 grams protein, 21 grams carbohydrate, no cholesterol, 123 calories.

Chili-spiced Bean Salad

This spicy variation on the three-bean salad theme includes corn and green chilies. You can pour the chili-seasoned dressing over the salad and chill it overnight, if you like.

   Chili Dressing (recipe follows)
   1 **can (1 lb. *each*) red kidney beans, pinto beans, and garbanzos**
   1 **can (1 lb.) whole kernel corn**
   1 **large stalk celery, thinly sliced**
   5 **green onions (including tops), thinly sliced**
   ¼ **cup chopped parsley**
   1 **can (4 oz.) diced green chilies**
   Lettuce leaves

Prepare dressing and reserve.

   Drain kidney beans, pinto beans, and garbanzos into a colander, rinse with cold water, drain, and turn into a salad bowl. Drain corn; add to beans along with celery, green onions, parsley, and chilies. Pour over dressing and mix lightly. Cover and refrigerate for 4 hours or until next day. Stir lightly before serving. Garnish with lettuce leaves. Makes 8 servings.

Per serving (including dressing): 13 grams protein, 44 grams carbohydrate, no cholesterol, 354 calories.

Chili Dressing. In a bowl, combine ¾ cup **salad oil**, ¼ cup **wine vinegar**, 1 clove **garlic** (minced or pressed), 1 teaspoon *each* **salt, chili powder,** and **oregano** leaves, ¼ teaspoon ground **cumin,** and a dash of **pepper.** Stir to blend well.

Lemon-Yogurt Dressing

Here's a low-calorie boiled dressing that's delightful on fruit salads.

Display a variety of fruit—melon crescents, pineapple spears, orange slices, pear quarters, grapes—in rows on a serving platter and offer the dressing in a separate bowl.

   ½ **cup sugar**
   1 **tablespoon cornstarch**
   ¼ **teaspoon salt**
   ⅔ **cup water**
   1 **teaspoon grated lemon peel**
   ⅓ **cup lemon juice**
   2 **eggs**
   1 **cup plain yogurt**

In a pan, blend sugar, cornstarch, and salt. Stir in water, lemon peel, and lemon juice. Cook, stirring, over medium heat until mixture boils and thickens.

   In a small bowl, lightly beat eggs. Stir some of the hot sauce into eggs, then stir all into mixture in pan; heat, stirring, for 1 minute. Remove from heat and cool for 10 minutes, stirring occasionally. Cover and refrigerate for as long as 5 days. Just before serving, fold in yogurt. Makes about 2 cups

Per tablespoon: .6 grams protein, 4 grams carbohydrate, 16 milligrams cholesterol, 22 calories.

Lemon-Thyme Dressing

You use lemon juice instead of vinegar to mingle with thyme and lots of minced parsley in this refreshing dressing. It's perfect on salad greens.

   ½ **cup salad oil**
   1½ **teaspoons grated lemon peel**
   ¼ **cup lemon juice**
   1 **small clove garlic, minced or pressed**
   1¼ **teaspoons sugar**
   ¾ **teaspoon thyme leaves**
   ½ **teaspoon salt**
   ⅛ **teaspoon pepper**
   ⅓ **cup chopped parsley**

In a container, combine oil, lemon peel, lemon juice, garlic, sugar, thyme, salt, and pepper; blend well. Just before serving, stir in parsley. Cover and refrigerate for as long as 1 week. Makes about 1 cup.

Per tablespoon: .07 grams protein, .8 grams carbohydrate, no cholesterol, 63 calories.

Toasted Sesame Seed Dressing

This nutlike dressing is good on any simple mixed green salad. For fewer calories, use sour half-and-half in place of sour cream.

   2 **tablespoons sesame seeds**
   ¼ **cup olive oil or salad oil**
   1 **tablespoon *each* lemon juice and honey**
   1 **teaspoon curry powder**
   1 **cup sour cream or sour half-and-half**
   Salt and pepper

Spread sesame seeds in a frying pan and cook over medium heat, shaking pan occasionally, until seeds turn golden and begin to pop (2 to 3 minutes); let cool.

   In a container, stir together oil, lemon juice, honey, toasted sesame seeds, curry, sour cream, and salt and pepper to taste. Cover and refrigerate for at least 1 hour or as long as 5 days. Makes about 1½ cups.

Per tablespoon (made with sour cream): .4 grams protein, .5 grams carbohydrate, 4 milligrams cholesterol, 44 calories.

***Artichoke marinade** acts like the genie in the jar for Quick Artichoke Pasta Salad (recipe on page 21), granting your wish for a well-seasoned instant salad dressing. It's delicious served with wedges of Zucchini Frittata (recipe on page 37).*

Soups for Starters or Full Meals

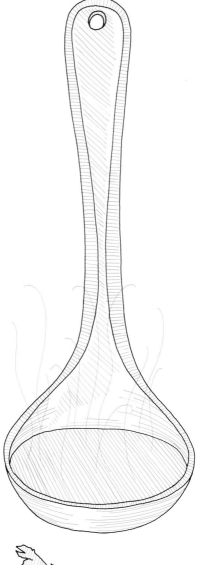

Discovering—or rediscovering—homemade soup is one of the delights of vegetarian cooking. That's why we've included a chapter devoted to soups of all kinds: meal-in-a-bowl soups, soups high in protein, soups packed with vegetables, soups that are creamy or spicy or chilled. This chapter is, in short, a veritable celebration of soups.

Of course, serving soup isn't obligatory, but we find that a meatless menu naturally places more emphasis on breads, salads, and soups.

Selecting a soup to go with two or three other vegetarian dishes is just a matter of exercising your good food sense. Nutrition, flavor, texture, and your own préferences are the most important considerations. For instance, it makes good sense to serve a tomato-based chunky vegetable soup with a smooth egg and cheese dish, rather than with a tomato-based chunky vegetable dish. This vegetable soup provides vitamins and minerals as well as some protein; the cheese and egg dish contains a large amount of complete protein.

If you do want to serve two vegetable dishes and avoid cheese and eggs, see to it that one dish contains legumes and the other a grain to make a complete protein. You might purée the soup to provide a contrasting texture, and sprinkle sunflower seeds or nuts on top. Of

course, you wouldn't season everything with the same herbs or to the same degree. Remember, the same esthetic principles apply for meals as for any sensuous event; sameness is monotonous; contrast is exciting. As for nutrition, the breakdown (per serving) of protein, carbohydrate, cholesterol, and calories at the end of each recipe provides some guidelines for menu planning.

Some soups are substantial enough to be the entrée, with only a light salad and perhaps some bread to round out the meal. And if you serve soup as a solo dish for supper, you serve up a bit of word history—at root, soup and supper are the same.

One of our favorite solo soups, the colorful Aztec Soup (page 32), starts with a simple base of corn and squash. Each guest then adds to his or her bowl from an assortment of condiments—fried tortilla strips, pine nuts, grated cheese, pumpkin seeds, diced avocado.

Of course, any main-dish soup can be served in small portions as part of an ensemble of vegetarian foods. The converse doesn't always work as well, though. Some soups, such as Potato Yogurt Soup (page 28), wouldn't be filling enough for a whole meal. Others, such as Chilled Cucumber Soup (page 35), would be too rich to serve in large portions.

Vegetarian Soup Stocks

Most of the soup recipes in this chapter call for a vegetable stock. The quickest way to prepare the amount of stock you'll need is to buy instant vegetable stock base in cubes or granules (labeled as vegetable-flavored instant bouillon or vegetarian-style instant bouillon).

For each cup of vegetable stock specified in our recipes, dissolve 1 teaspoon vegetable-flavored granules or 1 cube vegetable stock base in 1 cup boiling water.

If you have a little more time, you might want to try the recipe for Quick Vegetable Stock that follows. And, if you're inclined to be super-thrifty, you can save vegetable peelings and make a grand soup stock following the suggestions for Save-It-Up Vegetable Stock.

Quick Vegetable Stock. Made from fresh vegetables, this stock takes much less cooking time than meat stock. Here's the traditional French way to prepare a flavorful all-vegetable stock. Scrub and coarsely chop 3 large **carrots,** 1 large **turnip,** and 2 stalks **celery.** Peel and chop 2 large **onions.** Melt 2 tablespoons **butter** in an 8-quart pan over medium-high heat. Add chopped vegetables and cook, stirring occasionally, until vegetables turn golden (about 15 minutes).

Add 3 quarts **water,** 2 teaspoons **salt,** 6 large sprigs **parsley,** ½ **bay leaf,** and 1 teaspoon **thyme leaves.**

Cover and bring to a boil. Reduce heat and simmer for 1½ hours. Strain and discard vegetables. Makes 2½ quarts stock.

You can adjust the seasoning to suit your taste by adding 2 cloves peeled garlic, several peppercorns, or your favorite herbs. You can freeze extra stock for future soups.

Save-It-Up Vegetable Stock. This too is a thrifty, delicious base for soups. You make it by cooking the parings and trimmings saved from vegetables served during the week. You can also save up the cooking water from boiled or steamed vegetables—it's full of vitamins and minerals.

Save cooking and soaking water in a covered container in the refrigerator or freezer. Save parings and trimmings in a large plastic bag in the refrigerator.

Since most soup recipes in this chapter are best with a mildly flavored stock, you'll probably want to avoid using trimmings from pungent vegetables, such as cabbage and broccoli. Here are a few save-up suggestions: tips of green beans; ends of zucchini, crookneck squash, mushrooms, carrots, and asparagus stalks; potato peels, parsley stems, tomato trimmings, pea pods, wilted celery stalks, green onion tops, green pepper stems and seeds, wilted or outer leaves of lettuce, and spinach and chard stems.

When you have a quart or more of parings and trimmings, coarsely chop them, then place in a large pan and cover with cold water (or cover with the cooking water you've saved). The more chopped vegetable bits and pieces you use in proportion to the water, the stronger the stock. Salt lightly to bring out the flavor, then bring to a boil. Reduce heat; cover and simmer for 30 minutes.

If you want, you can add herbs to the stock—half a bay leaf, a pinch of thyme, a sprig of parsley. For a double-strength vegetable broth, you can use the save-it-up vegetable stock in place of water when you make the quick vegetable stock.

Almond Soup Gratinée

A large bowl of almond soup bubbling under a golden crust of cheese makes a heart-warming meal on a wintry day. You can prepare the broth ahead of time, but once you combine it with the eggs, you should complete the final steps.

Then you might serve it with a platter of Greek-style marinated vegetables (page 16) or a crisp green salad and a light red wine.

> About 1 tablespoon butter or
> margarine
> 4 slices French bread, cut
> ¾ inch thick
> 1 cup blanched slivered
> almonds
> 2 large cloves garlic, minced or
> pressed
> 6 cups vegetable stock
> (recipe at left)
> Salt and pepper
> 2 eggs
> 1 cup (4 oz.) shredded Swiss or
> Gruyère cheese
> Paprika

Butter both sides of bread and place in a single layer on a baking sheet. Bake in a 350° oven for 10 minutes or until bread is lightly browned; turn and lightly brown the other side.

Meanwhile, reserving 1 tablespoon of the almonds, spread remaining almonds in a shallow pan and toast in a 350° oven for about 8 minutes or until lightly browned. Let cool until crisp, then whirl with garlic in a blender or food processor until nuts are very finely chopped.

Place nuts in a 3-quart pan; add stock. Bring to a boil, then cover and simmer for 15 minutes. Add salt and pepper to taste. Beat eggs lightly. Remove soup from heat and, stirring constantly, stir eggs into soup.

Ladle hot soup into 4 individual ovenproof soup bowls (2 to 2½-cup size). Set a piece of toasted French bread on top of soup in each bowl and sprinkle equally with shredded cheese, the reserved almonds, and paprika.

Place bowls in a 425° oven for 10 minutes; then broil about 4 inches from heat until cheese and almonds brown. Makes 4 servings.

Per serving: 29 grams protein, 27 grams carbohydrate, 212 milligrams cholesterol, 488 calories.

Finnish Summer Soup

(Pictured on facing page)

Summer's most tender offerings—petite new peas, baby carrots, tiny onions, new potatoes—bob in a light cream soup. For a luncheon, you could serve moderate-size portions of this delightful soup with an array of decorated open-faced sandwiches. For supper you could serve larger portions accompanied by a bread-and-cheese platter.

2 cups water
4 to 6 small thin-skinned potatoes, peeled and halved
1 teaspoon salt
⅛ teaspoon white pepper
2 tablespoons butter or margarine
6 small boiling onions, or 6 green onions (including tops), cut into 3-inch lengths
12 very young fresh baby carrots (½ pound) or 1 package (8 oz.) frozen whole baby carrots
½ pound fresh young green beans, cut into 1-inch lengths, or 1 package (9 oz.) frozen cut green beans
2 cups fresh, shelled, tiny peas or 1 package (10 oz.) frozen tiny green peas
2 cups half-and-half (light cream)
3 tablespoons all-purpose flour

Heat water to boiling in a wide 5-quart pan; add potatoes. Reduce heat; cover and simmer for 5 minutes. Add salt, pepper, butter, onions, carrots, and green beans; simmer for 8 more minutes. Add peas and cook for another 2 minutes or until vegetables are crisp-tender.

Finnish Summer Soup (recipe above) features tender-crisp baby vegetables in light cream. Perfect post-sauna soup partners are open-faced sandwiches of cream cheese on rye, decorated with sliced vegetables.

In a small bowl, stir together half-and-half and flour until smooth; stir into simmering vegetables. Cook, stirring, until soup is slightly thickened (about 5 minutes). Makes five 1⅔-cup servings.

Per serving: 9 grams protein, 34 grams carbohydrate, 49 milligrams cholesterol, 292 calories.

Double Mushroom Soup

"It's like sipping the essence of mushrooms!" That's our favorite reaction to this fragrant soup. You make it with both dried and fresh mushrooms and just a touch of garlic, paprika, and thyme. Your guests will enjoy sipping this soup while waiting for a soufflé to finish cooking.

½ cup dried mushrooms
1 cup warm water
About 3 cups vegetable stock (page 25)
2 tablespoons butter or margarine
1 small onion, coarsely chopped
1 clove garlic, minced or pressed
½ pound fresh mushrooms, sliced
3 tablespoons all-purpose flour
½ teaspoon paprika
¼ teaspoon thyme leaves
Salt
About ⅓ cup plain yogurt or sour cream

Cover dried mushrooms with water and let stand for 30 minutes. Remove mushrooms; cut off and discard stems. Thinly slice mushrooms and set aside. Measure soaking water (discarding any sandy portion at the bottom) and add enough stock to make a total of 4 cups liquid; reserve.

In a 3-quart pan over medium-high heat, melt butter. Add onion, garlic, and fresh mushrooms; cook, stirring occasionally, until vegetables are golden and pan juices have evaporated. Stir in flour, paprika, and thyme. Add reserved stock mixture and dried mushrooms. Cook, stirring, until soup thickens slightly. Reduce heat; cover and simmer for 30 minutes.

In a blender or food processor, purée soup, a portion at a time, until smooth. Add salt to taste. Garnish each serving with a spoonful of yogurt or sour cream. Makes four 1-cup servings.

Per serving: 3 grams protein, 12 grams carbohydrate, 26 milligrams cholesterol, 146 calories.

Creamy Herbed Walnut Soup

An exquisite walnut flavor tinged with thyme and basil makes this soup a sophisticated first course, to be followed, perhaps, by a butter-lettuce salad and your favorite quiche.

1½ cups coarsely chopped walnuts
Water
2 cups milk
½ bay leaf
¼ teaspoon *each* thyme leaves and dry basil
2 tablespoons chopped parsley
2 tablespoons butter or margarine
1 medium-size onion, sliced
1 large stalk celery, thinly sliced
2 tablespoons whole wheat flour
3 cups vegetable stock (page 25)
2 tablespoons dry sherry
Salt and pepper
Finely chopped chives or green onion

In a pan over medium heat, cover walnuts with water and bring to a boil; boil for 3 minutes. Drain, rinse with cold water, and drain again. Pour milk over drained nuts and add bay, thyme, basil, and parsley; heat to scalding. Cover and set aside for 20 minutes.

Meanwhile, in a 3-quart pan over medium heat, melt butter. Add onion and celery and cook, stirring occasionally, for 5 minutes. Stir in flour and cook for 1 more minute. Gradually stir in stock; cook, stirring, until soup boils. Reduce heat; simmer for 10 minutes.

Remove bay leaf from milk-nut mixture; add mixture to soup. In a blender or food processor, purée soup, a portion at a time, until smooth. Return soup to pan and stir in sherry. Add salt and pepper to taste. Reheat without boiling.

Sprinkle each serving with chives. Makes seven 1-cup servings.

Per serving: 7 grams protein, 10 grams carbohydrate, 20 milligrams cholesterol, 255 calories.

Curried Peanut Soup

Since this soup contains an unusual combination of flavors, we expected a mixed reaction from our taste-testers. But they were enthusiastic: "It's wonderful! The crunchy peanuts on top and the mild curry flavor are marvelous."

It's an easy soup to make, especially if you have a cup of cooked brown rice left from another meal.

3 **tablespoons butter or margarine**
1 **small onion, finely chopped**
1 **medium-size carrot, finely chopped**
1 **large stalk celery, finely chopped**
1 **teaspoon curry powder**
2 **tablespoons whole wheat flour**
4 **cups vegetable stock (page 25)**
½ **cup peanut butter**
2 **tablespoons catsup**
2 **teaspoons Worcestershire**
1 **cup cooked brown rice**
About ½ cup *each* sour cream and chopped peanuts

In a 3-quart pan over medium heat, melt butter. Add onion, carrot, and celery and cook, stirring occasionally, until vegetables are soft (about 10 minutes). Stir in curry powder and cook for 1 minute. Stir in flour and cook for 1 more minute. Gradually stir in stock. Reduce heat; cover and simmer for 15 minutes.

Stir in peanut butter, catsup, and Worcestershire until smooth. Add rice and simmer, uncovered, for 5 minutes. Garnish each serving with a spoonful of sour cream and peanuts. Makes four 1⅓-cup servings.

Per serving: 12 grams protein, 20 grams carbohydrate, 35 milligrams cholesterol, 414 calories.

Cheddar Sherry Soup

Here you are in an intimate country inn ... mellow candlelight, a table to one side of a glowing hearth. For openers, the innkeeper suggests a bowl of Cheddar Sherry Soup —perfect. Can you have the recipe?

The innkeeper is only too happy to share the recipe (below). Don't forget the port and walnuts for dessert.

4 **tablespoons butter or margarine**
1 **large stalk celery, finely chopped**
1 **large carrot, finely chopped**
3 **green onions (including tops), thinly sliced**
3 **tablespoons all-purpose flour**
3 **cups vegetable stock (page 25)**
1 **cup milk**
2 **cups (8 oz.) shredded sharp Cheddar cheese**
¼ **cup dry or cream sherry**
White pepper
Ground nutmeg
Chopped parsley

In a 3-quart pan over medium heat, melt butter. Add celery and carrot and cook, stirring occasionally, for 5 minutes. Add onions and cook for 3 minutes. Stir in flour and cook for 1 more minute. Gradually stir in stock and cook, stirring, until soup thickens slightly. Reduce heat; cover and simmer for 10 minutes.

Add milk and cheese to soup and cook, stirring, until cheese is melted. Add sherry, then stir in pepper and nutmeg to taste. Garnish with chopped parsley. Makes four 1¼-cup servings.

Per serving: 17 grams protein, 12 grams carbohydrate, 100 milligrams cholesterol, 403 calories.

Potato Yogurt Soup

One of the light classics in our soup repertoire, Potato Yogurt Soup is a sprightly prelude to either an egg-and-cheese entrée or a vegetable-and-grain main course. Cucumber and lettuce are the surprise ingredients that add a touch of spring to this puréed soup.

3 tablespoons butter or margarine

1 cucumber, peeled, seeded, and cut into thick slices

3 medium-size thin-skinned potatoes, peeled and cut into 1-inch chunks

2 cups coarsely sliced lettuce

4 green onions (including tops), thinly sliced

3 cups vegetable stock (page 25)

1 teaspoon dill weed

1½ cups milk

2 tablespoons cornstarch

1 cup plain yogurt

Salt and white pepper

Fresh dill sprigs or chopped parsley

In a 3-quart pan over medium heat, melt butter. Add cucumber and potatoes and cook, stirring, for 4 minutes. Add lettuce, onions, stock, and the 1 teaspoon dill. Simmer, covered, until potatoes are tender (about 25 minutes).

In a blender or food processor, purée soup, a portion at a time, until smooth. Return to pan and stir in milk.

In a small bowl, combine cornstarch and yogurt; stir into soup. Cook, stirring, over medium heat, until hot and thickened. Season to taste with salt and pepper.

Garnish each serving with a sprig of fresh dill or a sprinkling of chopped parsley. Makes six 1⅓-cup servings.

Per serving: 5 grams protein, 20 grams carbohydrate, 26 milligrams cholesterol, 175 calories.

Hot & Sour Soup

White pepper makes it hot; vinegar makes it sour. This piquant hot-sour combination is a gift to the world's treasury of great soups from the Szechwan region of China. You can use the soup as a warmup for an Oriental feast, or serve it as the main event.

½ cup dried mushrooms

1 cup warm water

About 3 cups vegetable stock (page 25)

1 tablespoon dry sherry

½ cup sliced bamboo shoots, cut in matchstick pieces, or ½ cup sliced water chestnuts

4 ounces tofu, diced

½ cup frozen peas, thawed

2 tablespoons white wine vinegar

1 tablespoon soy sauce

2 tablespoons cornstarch

¼ cup water

½ to ¾ teaspoon white pepper

1 teaspoon sesame oil

1 egg, lightly beaten

2 green onions (including tops), cut into 1-inch diagonal slices

Salt

Cover mushrooms with water and let stand for 30 minutes. Remove mushrooms; cut off and discard stems. Thinly slice mushrooms and set aside. Measure soaking water (discard any sandy portion at the bottom) and add enough stock to make a total of 4 cups liquid. Place in a 2-quart pan and add sherry, bamboo shoots, and sliced mushrooms. Bring to a boil, then reduce heat; cover and simmer for 15 minutes. Add tofu, peas, wine vinegar, and soy; heat for 3 minutes.

In a small bowl, stir together cornstarch and the ¼ cup water. Add to soup and cook, stirring, until slightly thickened. Turn off heat. Add pepper and sesame oil. Stirring continuously, slowly pour egg into soup. Sprinkle with onion; add salt to taste. Makes four 1½-cup servings.

Per serving: 6 grams protein, 10 grams carbohydrate, 63 milligrams cholesterol, 95 calories.

Tomato Corn Chowder

Here's a marvelous summertime chowder, mellow and sweet from the freshest corn you can find. Removing the corn kernels is messy, but not difficult. You can serve this pretty and filling soup with thick slices of whole wheat bread and a fruit salad with cottage cheese.

4 large ears corn on the cob

3 tablespoons butter or margarine

1 medium-size onion, chopped

1 clove garlic, minced or pressed

1 stalk celery, thinly sliced

1 large carrot, thinly sliced

2 small potatoes, peeled and diced

3 medium-size tomatoes, seeded and coarsely chopped

1 teaspoon salt

¼ teaspoon white pepper

½ teaspoon dry basil

3 cups vegetable stock (page 25)

1 cup half-and-half (light cream)

About ½ cup alfalfa sprouts or chopped parsley

With a sharp knife, cut corn off cob, leaving kernel bases attached. With back of knife, scrape cob to extract the creamy pulp. Reserve.

In a 5-quart pan over medium heat, melt butter. Add onion, garlic, celery, and carrot; cook, stirring occasionally, until vegetables are soft (about 10 minutes). Add potatoes, tomatoes, salt, pepper, basil, stock, and reserved corn to pan. Reduce heat; cover and simmer until potatoes are fork-tender (about 30 minutes). Add half-and-half and heat through without boiling. Garnish each serving with sprouts or parsley. Makes six 1⅔-cup servings.

Per serving: 5 grams protein, 24 grams carbohydrate, 35 milligrams cholesterol, 204 calories.

Soybean Soup, Bistro-style

With protein-packed, cooked soybeans from your freezer, you can make a quick meal that needs only the accompaniment of green salad and whole wheat bread.

        6 medium-size leeks, or 2
          medium-size onions,
          chopped
        3 tablespoons butter or
          margarine
        1 small onion, chopped
        1 large stalk celery, sliced
        1 medium-size carrot, thinly
          sliced
        1 medium-size turnip, peeled
          and diced
     2½ cups cooked soybeans,
          (page 49)
        4 cups vegetable stock
          (page 25)
        ¼ teaspoon thyme leaves
          Salt and white pepper
        1 cup milk or half-and-half
          (light cream)
        ¼ cup chopped watercress or
          parsley
          Lemon slices

Trim root ends and tough outer leaves from leeks. Slit each leek lengthwise, rinse between layers, then thinly slice.

In a 5-quart pan over medium heat, melt butter. Add leeks and onion (or use all onion), celery, and carrot. Cook, stirring, until onion is soft (about 10 minutes). Add turnip, soybeans, stock, and thyme. Reduce heat; cover and simmer until vegetables are tender (about 40 minutes).

In a blender or food processor, purée soup, a portion at a time, until smooth. Return soup to pan. Add salt and pepper to taste. Stir in milk and reheat without boiling. Garnish with watercress and lemon slices. Makes six 1⅓-cup servings.

Per serving: 11 grams protein, 19 grams carbohydrate, 23 milligrams cholesterol, 212 calories.

Cuban Black Bean Soup

For a light meal, accompany this soup with cheese-topped corn tortillas. For a larger feast, offer portions of the soup as a first course to be followed by enchiladas or chiles rellenos.

          Marinated Rice (directions
          follow)
        4 tablespoons olive oil or
          salad oil
        2 medium-size onions, finely
          chopped
        2 medium-size green peppers,
          seeded and finely chopped
        5 large cloves garlic, minced or
          pressed
          About 3 cups vegetable stock
          (page 25)
     1½ teaspoons *each* ground
          cumin and oregano leaves
        2 tablespoons vinegar
          About 6 cups cooked black or
          red beans (page 49)
          Salt

Prepare marinated rice. Set aside for 1 hour or until next day; bring to room temperature before serving.

Heat oil in a 5-quart pan over medium heat. Add onions, green peppers, and garlic; cook, stirring, until limp. Add stock, cumin, oregano, vinegar, and beans. Cover and simmer for 30 minutes, adding more stock if desired for thinner consistency. Add salt to taste.

Serve in bowls, adding a generous spoonful of the cool rice to each bowl of hot soup. Makes six 1⅔-cup servings.

Per serving: 17 grams protein, 60 grams carbohydrate, no cholesterol, 467 calories.

Marinated Rice. Thinly slice 3 **green onions** (including tops). Combine with 2 cups cooked **white rice**, 1 **tomato** (finely chopped), and 3 tablespoons *each* **olive oil** and **white wine vinegar.** Cover and chill.

Lemony Lentil Soup

Lemon is the perfect accent for lentils and Swiss chard—the main ingredients in this meal-in-a bowl soup from Lebanon. Enjoy it as an entrée accompanied by black bread and cucumbers with yogurt.

     1½ cups lentils
        8 cups vegetable stock
          (page 25)
        1 large potato
        2 bunches (about 1½ pounds)
          Swiss chard
        1 medium-size onion, finely
          chopped
        4 tablespoons olive oil or salad
          oil
        ½ cup coarsely chopped fresh
          coriander (cilantro), or ½ cup
          chopped parsley plus ¾
          teaspoon ground coriander
        3 cloves garlic, minced or
          pressed
          Salt
        ¼ teaspoon pepper
        ½ teaspoon ground cumin
        3 tablespoons lemon juice
          Lemon slices

Rinse lentils; sort through and discard any foreign material. Drain well. Combine lentils and stock in an 8-quart pan; cover and bring to simmering.

Peel potato and cut into ½-inch cubes; add to lentils. Cover and simmer for 20 minutes. Slice chard leaves and stems crosswise in ½-inch wide strips. Add to soup, cover, and continue simmering until lentils are tender (about 20 more minutes).

(Continued on page 32)

Razzle-dazzle your taste buds with Sweet & Sour Borscht (recipe on page 33). Then follow the ruby-red soup with plump Potato-Onion Blintzes (recipe on page 56) topped with sour cream, green onion slices, and poppy seeds.

In a small frying pan over medium heat, cook onion in oil, stirring occasionally, until onion is soft and golden (about 10 minutes). Add to onion ⅓ cup of the fresh coriander (or ⅓ cup of the parsley-coriander mixture) along with garlic and cook for 1 to 2 minutes.

Add onion mixture to soup during the last 5 minutes of cooking. Stir in salt to taste, pepper, cumin, and lemon juice. Garnish soup with lemon slices and remaining chopped coriander or parsley-coriander mixture. Makes six 1⅔-cup servings.

Per serving: 16 grams protein, 43 grams carbohydrate, no cholesterol, 310 calories.

Broccoli Barley Soup

Thick enough to be called a porridge, but full of the fresh taste of broccoli and rosemary, this is a good soup to serve on a brisk day. You could present it with an egg dish for a substantial dinner, or serve it with bread and cheese for a lighter supper.

- **3 tablespoons butter or margarine**
- **2 medium-size onions, chopped**
- **2 cloves garlic, minced or pressed**
- **¼ pound mushrooms, sliced**
- **½ teaspoon dry rosemary**
- **6 cups vegetable stock (page 25)**
- **¾ cup pearl barley**
- **1 pound broccoli**
- **2 tablespoons cornstarch**
- **¼ cup water**
- **2 cups milk**
  Salt and pepper
  About ⅓ cup grated Parmesan cheese

In a 5-quart pan over medium-high heat, melt butter. Add onions, gar-lic, and mushrooms. Cook, stirring frequently, until onion is soft (about 5 minutes). Add rosemary, stock, and barley and bring to a boil. Reduce heat; cover and simmer until barley is tender (about 45 minutes).

Meanwhile, remove broccoli flowerets and cut into bite-size pieces. Peel stems and thinly slice. When barley is tender, increase heat and add broccoli stems and pieces. Cook, covered, until broccoli is just tender and still bright green (about 10 minutes).

In a small bowl, stir together cornstarch and water. Add to soup along with milk and cook, stirring, until soup boils and thickens. Add salt and pepper to taste. Sprinkle each serving lightly with Parmesan cheese. Makes six 1⅔-cup servings.

Per serving: 10 grams protein, 36 grams carbohydrate, 33 milligrams cholesterol, 265 calories.

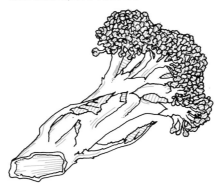

Aztec Soup

By far the most unusual soup in this chapter, Aztec Soup glows with the golden-orange colors of squash and corn. And that's just the basic soup—the background, as it were. At the table you pass bowls of condiments (pine nuts, walnuts, fried tortilla pieces, grated cheese, pumpkin seeds, diced avocado) and let family or guests compose their own soup to suit their individual tastes.

To complete the meal, you might want to include a bowl of refried beans; fresh fruit would be excellent for dessert.

Fried Tortilla Pieces (directions follow)
- **3 tablespoons butter or margarine**
- **⅔ cup (about 3 oz.) pine nuts**
- **¾ cup walnut halves**
- **1 large onion, coarsely chopped**
- **2 cloves garlic, minced or pressed**
- **12 cups vegetable stock (page 25)**
- **4 cups diced, peeled butternut, acorn, or hubbard squash**
- **2 packages (10 oz. *each*) frozen corn**
- **¾ cup toasted shelled pumpkin seeds**
- **1 large avocado**
- **3 cups (12 oz.) shredded jack cheese**

Fry tortilla pieces.

In an 8-quart pan over medium heat, melt 1 tablespoon of the butter. Add pine nuts and walnuts and cook, stirring, until golden (about 2 minutes). Remove nuts; reserve.

Melt the remaining 2 tablespoons butter in pan and cook onion and garlic until onion is golden. Add stock and squash and bring to boiling. Reduce heat; cover and simmer until squash is tender (10 to 15 minutes). Add corn and cook for 5 more minutes. Sprinkle with pumpkin seeds just before serving. Peel and dice avocado.

Arrange avocado, reserved nuts, cheese, and tortilla pieces in bowls. Pass condiments at the table to add to the soup. Makes ten 2-cup servings.

Per serving (including tortillas): 20 grams protein, 38 grams carbohydrate, 44 milligrams cholesterol, 543 calories.

Fried Tortilla Pieces. Arrange 8 **corn tortillas** in a stack and cut into 6 equal wedges. Pour about ½ inch **salad oil** in a deep 2 or 3-quart pan and set on medium-high to high heat. When oil is hot enough to make a piece of tortilla sizzle, add tortilla pieces, a handful at a time, and stir to separate. Cook until crisp (1 to 1½ minutes); lift from oil with slotted spoon and drain on paper towels.

Garden Fresh Minestrone

Minestrone means "big soup," and that's exactly what this recipe makes—a generous quantity of main-dish soup. While minestrone is a traditional dish, there is no definitive way to prepare it. The best minestrone is the one filled with your family's favorite seasonal vegetables.

3 medium-size leeks, or 1 medium-size onion, chopped

2 cloves garlic, minced or pressed

3 tablespoons olive oil or salad oil

8 cups vegetable stock (page 25)

1 can (1 pound) kidney beans

6 cups prepared fresh vegetables (such as diced turnips and potatoes; sliced carrots, celery, zucchini, and crookneck squash; green beans cut in 1-inch lengths; and shelled peas)

½ teaspoon *each* dry basil, oregano leaves, and dry rosemary

¼ cup tomato paste

½ cup elbow macaroni

2 cups shredded cabbage, spinach, or chard

Salt and pepper

About ½ cup grated Parmesan cheese

Trim root ends and tough outer leaves from leeks; slit each leek lengthwise, rinse between layers, then thinly slice.

In a 6-quart kettle over medium heat, cook leeks and garlic in oil, stirring occasionally, for 5 minutes. Add stock, beans and their liquid, vegetables, basil, oregano, and rosemary; bring to simmering.

Reduce heat; cover and cook for 30 minutes.

Stir in tomato paste and macaroni and continue simmering for 15 minutes or until macaroni is tender. Add cabbage and cook, covered, just until it wilts (about 5 more minutes). Season to taste with salt and pepper. Pass Parmesan at the table. Makes eight 2-cup servings.

Per serving: 11 grams protein, 36 grams carbohydrate, 5 milligrams cholesterol, 243 calories.

Sweet & Sour Borscht

(Pictured on page 31)

This jewel of a soup shimmers with the ruby-red of beets and the bright vermilion of carrots. You can serve it with cheese and black bread for lunch or a light supper; or serve it before a main course like blintzes.

3 medium-size beets with leafy tops

2 tablespoons salad oil

1 small onion, chopped

2 large carrots, diced

2 cups coarsely shredded red or green cabbage

¼ cup lemon juice

2½ tablespoons sugar

½ teaspoon dill weed

6 cups vegetable stock (page 25)

Salt and pepper

About ½ cup plain yogurt or sour cream

Cut off beet tops. Cut off and discard stems and any wilted leaves. Coarsely chop remaining leaves. Peel beets and shred coarsely; set aside.

Heat oil in a 5-quart pan over medium heat. Add onion and carrots and cook, stirring occasionally, until vegetables are soft (about 10 minutes). Add beets and tops, cabbage, lemon juice, sugar, dill, and

stock; bring to simmering. Reduce heat to low; cover and simmer until beets and cabbage are tender (about 45 minutes). Season with salt and pepper to taste.

Garnish each serving with yogurt. Makes six 1⅔-cup servings.

Per serving: 2 grams protein, 14 grams carbohydrate, 9 milligrams cholesterol, 137 calories.

Fresh Vegetable Basil Soup

(Pictured on page 34)

Chock-full of good crunchy vegetables, this soup speaks with an Italian accent. You might follow it with other Italian favorites, like an antipasto platter and a frittata.

3 tablespoons butter or margarine

1 medium-size onion, chopped

1 large stalk celery, sliced

1 large carrot, sliced ⅛-inch thick

1 large thin-skinned potato

2 large tomatoes

4 cups vegetable stock (page 25)

3 tablespoons coarsely chopped fresh basil or 1 teaspoon dry basil

½ small head cauliflower, broken into flowerets

2 small zucchini, sliced ¼ inch thick

½ pound fresh green peas, shelled

Salt and pepper

About ½ cup grated Parmesan cheese

In a 5-quart pan over medium heat, melt butter. Add onion, celery, and carrot; cook, stirring occasionally, until vegetables are soft but not brown (about 10 minutes).

Meanwhile, peel potato and cut into ½-inch cubes. Peel and dice tomatoes; you should have 2 cups. Add potato, tomatoes, stock, and

(Continued on page 35)

...Fresh Vegetable Basil Soup (cont'd.)

basil to pan. Bring to a boil, then cover and simmer for 15 minutes.

Add cauliflower and zucchini and simmer for 10 more minutes. Add peas and simmer for another 5 minutes or until all vegetables are tender. Season to taste with salt and pepper. Pass Parmesan cheese at the table to sprinkle onto soup. Makes six 1⅔-cup servings.

Per serving: 9 grams protein, 21 grams carbohydrate, 24 milligrams cholesterol, 178 calories.

Make-ahead Gazpacho ✓

It's a sip of cool pleasure on a sun-dappled day. It's a taste-tempting way to start a party. It's gazpacho, the easiest make-ahead soup a cook can concoct to begin a meal.

2 cups *each* vegetable stock (page 25) and tomato juice

2 tablespoons *each* lemon juice and green taco sauce

1 teaspoon sugar

½ teaspoon garlic salt

⅛ teaspoon pepper

1 cucumber, peeled, seeded, and coarsely chopped

1 green pepper, seeded and diced

4 large tomatoes, peeled and coarsely chopped

3 green onions (including tops), thinly sliced

In a 3-quart pan over medium heat, combine stock, tomato juice, lemon juice, taco sauce, sugar, garlic salt, and pepper. Leave uncovered and bring to a boil. Stir in cucumber, green pepper, tomatoes, and onion; bring mixture, uncovered, to a boil again. Remove from heat and cool. Cover

Abbondanza! That means abundance in Italian, and that's the word for Fresh Vegetable Basil Soup (recipe on page 33). It's made with an abundance of fresh vegetables and a rich seasoning of basil.

and refrigerate until well chilled. Makes six 1-cup servings.

Per serving: 3 grams protein, 14 grams carbohydrate, no cholesterol, 64 calories.

Almond Buttermilk Soup

If you were dining in Denmark, you might be served this lightly sweetened, chilled buttermilk soup topped with clouds of fluffy meringue and colorful berries.

2 cups berries (strawberries, raspberries, or blackberries)

Honey or sugar

2 eggs

¼ cup sugar

⅛ teaspoon almond extract

2½ cups buttermilk

¼ cup sliced almonds

Rinse berries, drain, and, if using strawberries, slice; set aside ½ cup to use as garnish. Put remaining berries in a serving bowl and drizzle with honey or sprinkle with sugar (about 1 tablespoon); set aside.

Separate eggs; put whites into a small bowl, yolks into a large bowl. Beat egg whites until fluffy. Gradually add 2 tablespoons of the sugar and continue to beat until the mixture holds stiff peaks; reserve.

Beat egg yolks until lemon colored; gradually add the remaining 2 tablespoons sugar along with almond extract. Beat until thick and smooth. Stir in buttermilk.

Pour buttermilk mixture over berries in serving bowl. Top with reserved egg whites and berries; garnish with almonds. Serve at once, or cover and chill up to 2 hours.

To serve, ladle soup and a portion of meringue and berries into each bowl. Makes four 1-cup servings.

Per serving: 11 grams protein, 28 grams carbohydrate, 129 milligrams cholesterol, 220 calories.

Chilled Cucumber Soup

You start this soup by making an unsweetened custard. Then whisk in sour cream and add finely chopped cucumber. As an opener for a warm-weather dinner, offer small glass bowls of this soup. Or serve it for lunch accompanied by toasted rye bread that's topped with sautéed mushrooms, covered with Swiss cheese, and broiled.

3 eggs

2 cups milk

1 cup sour cream

2 medium-size cucumbers

1 cup vegetable stock (page 25)

½ cup dry white wine

1 green onion (including top), finely chopped

1 tablespoon chopped pimento

½ teaspoon dill weed

Salt

About 2 tablespoons grated Parmesan cheese

In a small bowl, beat eggs lightly. In top of a double boiler over direct heat, heat milk to scalding. With a fork, gradually blend milk into eggs. Return mixture to top of double boiler, place over simmering water, and cook, stirring constantly, until custard coats a metal spoon in a velvety smooth layer. Remove from heat and cool. Stir sour cream into cooled custard.

Cut a dozen thin slices of unpeeled cucumber for garnish; reserve. Peel, seed, and finely chop remaining cucumber. Stir into custard mixture along with stock, wine, onion, pimento, and dill. Add salt to taste. Chill thoroughly.

Serve cold in small bowls. Garnish each serving with cucumber slices and a sprinkling of Parmesan cheese. Makes five 1-cup servings.

Per serving: 10 grams protein, 11 grams carbohydrate, 188 milligrams cholesterol, 238 calories.

Main Dishes with Eggs & Cheese

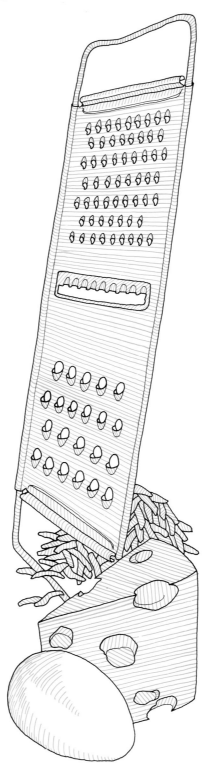

For the part-time vegetarian and anyone just looking for a change of pace from meat entrées, cheese and egg dishes are a natural choice. They're instantly appealing to the whole family—even confirmed meat eaters—and many of them are spectacular enough for party fare.

While there's nothing out of the ordinary about serving a plain omelet, soufflé, or quiche, you'll find this chapter's collection of recipes extraordinary. There's an open-faced Country Omelet (page 37) that's topped with a luscious mixture of diced potatoes, onions, Swiss cheese, and parsley, plus a scoop of sour cream and a crunchy garnish of walnut halves. Definitely out of the ordinary! But it's easy to make—you don't even have to fold the omelet; just cut it in wedges and serve it from the pan.

In the soufflé category, you'll find a Camembert Soufflé (page 40) that has the traditional high-rising shape, and a Broccoli Soufflé Roll (page 40) that's not only unusually delicious, but unusually shaped—it looks like a jelly roll.

The versatile quiche has four representatives in this chapter. Our Spinach & Feta Quiche (page 41) is a good choice to serve cold with a classic Greek salad. The Russian Quiche (page 42), chock-full of onions and mushrooms spiked with a

touch of horseradish, would be delicious paired with the Sweet & Sour Borscht (page 33). Or you might like to whip up the Golden Cauliflower Quiche baked in an oatmeal pastry shell (page 41), or go for a quiche with no pastry shell at all—the Mushroom Crust Quiche (page 42).

As a special feature, there's a section on homemade cheese and yogurt. We find making yogurt a great moneysaver, and the cheese made from yogurt is a revelation in tangy freshness. This feature also includes two recipes for raita (page 47)—a refreshing mixture of yogurt, chopped vegetables, and spices, that goes especially well with Indian curries.

Eggs contain an amazing amount of cholesterol—252 milligrams per large egg. If you should be limiting your intake of cholesterol, you'll want to limit the number of egg dishes you eat.

Many kinds of cheese, too, have substantial amounts of cholesterol (28 milligrams in 1 ounce of Swiss cheese) and a lot of calories (105 calories in 1 ounce of Swiss cheese). But with cheeses like Swiss, Cheddar, and jack, or hard cheese like Parmesan, a little can go a long way to add protein to your menu—not to mention calcium, an essential nutrient found in abundance in cheese.

Cheese & Basil Omelet

Basil is a wonderful herb to combine with eggs and cheese. In this recipe, you cook the egg mixture in butter and garlic, then sprinkle with basil and—surprise—blue cheese. For a quick family supper, you can serve this omelet with sliced tomatoes and Whole Wheat Crescent Rolls (page 73). For a heartier meal, you might start off with a bowl of Potato Yogurt Soup (page 28).

> 8 eggs
> 3 tablespoons water
> ½ teaspoon salt
> ¼ teaspoon pepper
> 2 tablespoons butter or margarine
> 1 large clove garlic, minced or pressed
> 3 ounces blue-veined cheese, coarsely crumbled
> 3 tablespoons chopped fresh basil leaves or 1 tablespoon dry basil

Beat eggs lightly with water, salt, and pepper.

Heat a 10-inch omelet pan or frying pan with sloping sides over medium-high heat. Add butter and garlic and stir until butter melts; tilt pan so butter coats bottom and sides. Pour in egg mixture and cook, gently lifting cooked portion to allow uncooked egg to flow underneath. Gently shake pan to keep omelet free.

When top of omelet is almost set but still moist, sprinkle with cheese and basil. Continue to shake pan and lift omelet edges until there is no more liquid, but top still looks moist and creamy.

Tilting pan over a serving plate, shake pan to slide half the omelet onto plate; with a flick of the wrist, fold over remaining omelet. Makes 4 servings.

Per serving: 18 grams protein, 2 grams carbohydrate, 542 milligrams cholesterol, 295 calories.

Country Omelet

This omelet is served from the frying pan and cut into wedges like a pie. The topping is scrumptious—a mixture of lightly browned diced potato, onions, Swiss cheese, and parsley, with a scoop of sour cream in the center. Don't forget our favorite part—a garnish of walnuts.

> 3 tablespoons butter or margarine
> ¼ cup walnut halves
> 1 small thin-skinned potato, diced
> ¼ cup chopped onion
> 4 eggs
> ¼ cup diced Swiss cheese
> 2 tablespoons shredded Swiss cheese
> 1 tablespoon chopped parsley
> Salt
> About ¼ cup sour cream

Melt 1½ tablespoons of the butter in a wide frying pan over medium heat. Add walnuts and cook until lightly browned (about 1 or 2 minutes). Remove nuts with a slotted spoon and set aside. Reduce heat to medium-low. Add potato and onion and cook, stirring, until potato is soft but only lightly browned (about 10 minutes). Remove from pan and set aside; keep warm.

Remove any particles from pan, then melt remaining 1½ tablespoons butter over medium-low heat. Beat eggs lightly; add to pan and cook, gently lifting cooked portion to allow uncooked egg to flow underneath. When top of omelet is almost set but still moist, sprinkle evenly with potato-onion mixture, diced cheese, shredded cheese, parsley, and salt to taste. Mound sour cream in center of omelet. Garnish with toasted walnuts.

Cut in wedges and serve from pan. Makes 4 servings.

Per serving: 16 grams protein, 10 grams carbohydrate, 307 milligrams cholesterol, 375 calories.

✓ Zucchini Frittata

(Pictured on page 23)

A frittata is a flat omelet with a medley of vegetables and herbs mixed into it. This recipe calls for zucchini and chard, but you can substitute any summer squash for the zucchini, and spinach for the chard.

> 2 tablespoons salad oil
> 1 small onion, finely chopped
> 1 clove garlic, minced or pressed
> 2 large Swiss chard leaves (including stems), coarsely chopped
> 1 medium-size zucchini, coarsely chopped
> 6 eggs
> ⅛ teaspoon pepper
> ¼ teaspoon *each* dry basil and oregano leaves
> 1 cup (3 oz.) grated Parmesan cheese

Heat oil in a wide frying pan over medium-high heat. Add onion, garlic, chard, and zucchini; cook, stirring occasionally, until vegetables are soft (about 5 minutes). Remove from heat and let cool slightly.

Beat eggs lightly with pepper, basil, and oregano. Stir in cheese and vegetables. Pour into a greased 9-inch pie pan. Bake in a 350° oven for 25 to 30 minutes or until puffed and browned. Serve hot or at room temperature. Makes 6 servings.

Per serving: 14 grams protein, 4 grams carbohydrate, 269 milligrams cholesterol, 204 calories.

Mayan Egg Tortillas

Toasted pumpkin seeds and chilies flavor the sauce for this delicious dish. You can prepare the sauce ahead of time and refrigerate it until time to spoon it over the lightly scrambled eggs wrapped in whole wheat tortillas. You may want to seve these tortillas with a platter of fresh fruit garnished with lime wedges, and mugs of hot cinnamon-spiced chocolate.

8 ounces (about 1½ cups) toasted shelled pumpkin seeds

½ cup vegetable stock (page 25)

3 tablespoons lemon juice

1 clove garlic, cut into thirds

3 tablespoons diced canned green chilies

½ teaspoon *each* salt and pepper

½ pint (1 cup) whipping cream

8 large whole wheat tortillas (page 81)

8 eggs

2 tablespoons milk

2 tablespoons butter or margarine

2 green onions (including tops), chopped

In a blender or food processor, whirl pumpkin seeds until coarsely chopped; turn out half the chopped seeds and set them aside. Add stock, lemon juice, garlic, chilies, salt, and pepper to remaining seeds and whirl until well mixed. Add cream and whirl briefly to blend. Stir in remaining seeds. If made ahead, cover sauce and refrigerate.

Stack tortillas, wrap in foil, and place in a 325° oven for 6 to 8 minutes or until heated through and softened. If tortillas are very fresh, do not heat them; just bring to room temperature.

Beat eggs lightly with milk. Melt butter in a wide frying pan over medium-low heat. Pour in egg mixture and cook, gently lifting cooked portion to allow uncooked egg to flow underneath, until eggs are barely set and top is still moist.

Spoon ⅛ of the scrambled eggs down center of each tortilla; top each with about 2 tablespoons of the sauce. Roll to enclose filling; arrange, seam side down, in a shal-

low baking dish. Spoon remaining sauce over top.

Broil 4 to 6 inches from heat until sauce is heated through and tortillas are flecked with brown. Sprinkle with green onions before serving. Makes 8 servings.

Per serving: 18 grams protein, 25 grams carbohydrate, 319 milligrams cholesterol, 500 calories.

Crunchy Egg Patties

Tofu goes international in this recipe. It combines with Italian and Chinese vegetables and turns up in small patties or frittatas. You can't taste the tofu, but it makes the egg mixture creamy and soft, and boosts the protein content.

About 8 ounces tofu

1 teaspoon *each* dry sherry and soy sauce

1 small stalk celery, chopped

1 green onion (including top), finely chopped

½ cup shredded zucchini

4 small mushrooms, thinly sliced

¼ pound bean sprouts

¾ teaspoon salt

Dash of pepper

2 tablespoons grated Parmesan cheese

6 eggs

Drain tofu and pat dry with paper towels. Crumble into a large bowl; stir in sherry and soy and let stand for 5 minutes. Add celery, onion, zucchini, mushrooms, bean sprouts, salt, pepper, and cheese; mix lightly. Lightly beat eggs, then stir into vegetable mixture.

Heat a griddle or large frying pan over medium-high heat; grease well. Spoon mixture, about ¼ cup for each patty, onto griddle. From the bowl, spoon about 2 more tablespoons of only the liquid egg over each patty and distribute

evenly over vegetables. Cook until egg is set and bottoms of patties are golden brown. Turn with a spatula and cook other sides until browned. Keep warm in a 200° oven until all patties are cooked. Makes 5 servings, 2 patties each.

Per serving: 13 grams protein, 3 grams carbohydrate, 305 milligrams cholesterol, 147 calories.

Puffy Herb Omelet

Beating egg whites and yolks separately makes a light, puffy omelet. After the herb-filled creation finishes cooking, you fold it in half and tuck in fresh sprouts—either alfalfa sprouts or blanched bean sprouts.

Cheddar Cheese Sauce (recipe follows)

5 eggs, separated

¼ cup milk

½ teaspoon salt

2 tablespoons chopped parsley

1 tablespoon chopped fresh or freeze-dried chives

1 teaspoon dill weed

¼ teaspoon *each* dry mustard, pepper, and garlic salt

1½ tablespoons butter or margarine

1 cup alfalfa sprouts

Prepare Cheddar Cheese Sauce.

Beat egg whites until stiff, moist peaks form. In a separate bowl,

(Continued on page 40)

For luscious simplicity, just top a round of brie with butter and sliced almonds, heat it until the cheese is hot and fluid, and serve it as an entrée. Your guests will relish their role— scooping up the melted cheese with French bread. Offer fruit, too— such as grapes, pears, and apples. The recipe for Baked Brie is on page 45.

beat egg yolks until very thick; stir in milk, salt, parsley, chives, dill weed, mustard, pepper, and garlic salt. Gently fold egg yolk mixture into whites until blended.

In a 10-inch omelet pan or frying pan with sloping sides and heat-resistant handle, melt butter over medium heat; tilt pan to coat bottom and sides. Pour egg mixture into pan and smooth surface gently. Reduce heat to low and cook until lightly browned on bottom (5 to 7 minutes); lift edge of omelet with a spatula to test.

Place pan in a 325° oven for 10 to 12 minutes or until a knife inserted in the center comes out clean.

Run a spatula around edge of omelet. Tip pan and slide spatula under omelet to loosen; fold omelet in half and slip onto a heated plate.

With a spatula, lift top edge gently and quickly tuck sprouts into fold. To serve, cut into wide slices; pass hot Cheddar Cheese Sauce at the table. Makes 4 servings.

Per serving (including cheese sauce): 11 grams protein, 5 grams carbohydrate, 334 milligrams cholesterol, 186 calories.

Cheddar Cheese Sauce. In a pan, combine 1 can (10¾ oz.) condensed **Cheddar cheese soup,** ¼ cup **milk** or dry white wine, and several dashes of **Worcestershire sauce.** Stir over medium heat until smooth and bubbly.

Camembert Soufflé

A bottle of champagne waiting on ice, soft music, a bouquet of sweetheart roses on the table... For that kind of mood, whether it be a late evening supper or a Sunday brunch, you need a special dish like Camembert Soufflé. Its extra rich taste and creamy texture come from just a small wedge of Camembert cheese.

Butter or margarine
Grated Parmesan cheese
4 **tablespoons butter or margarine**
¼ **teaspoon ground nutmeg**
⅛ **teaspoon ground red pepper (cayenne)**
3 **tablespoons all-purpose flour**
1⅓ **cups milk**
2 **teaspoons Dijon mustard**
2 **tablespoons dry sherry**
4 **ounces ripe Camembert cheese, rind removed**
1¼ **cups (5 oz.) shredded Gruyère, Samsoe, or Swiss cheese**
5 **eggs, separated**
¼ **teaspoon *each* cream of tartar and salt**

Preheat oven to 375°. Generously butter a 2-quart soufflé dish or casserole. Sprinkle with Parmesan cheese, turning dish to coat bottom and sides; set aside.

Melt the 4 tablespoons butter in a 3-quart pan over medium heat. Add nutmeg and red pepper. Blend in flour and cook, stirring, until bubbly. Gradually pour in milk and continue cooking and stirring until sauce boils and thickens. Add mustard, sherry, Camembert cheese, and Gruyère cheese; stir just until cheeses are melted. Set aside.

In a small bowl, beat egg yolks. Gradually stir ¼ cup of the cheese sauce into egg yolks, then stir mixture back into cheese sauce. Return to heat and cook, stirring, for 1 minute.

In a large bowl, combine egg whites, cream of tartar, and salt. Beat until short, moist peaks form. Fold ¼ cup of the beaten whites into cheese sauce. Slowly fold sauce into remaining whites. Pour into prepared soufflé dish.

Bake in the preheated 375° oven for 35 to 40 minutes or until top is browned and center feels firm when lightly touched. Serve immediately. Makes 6 servings.

Per serving: 17 grams protein, 4 grams carbohydrate, 286 milligrams cholesterol, 324 calories.

Broccoli Soufflé Roll

First you bake the egg mixture in a jelly roll pan until the egg is light and puffy. Then you spread it with a cheese-broccoli filling, roll it up, and—voilà!—an impressive entrée ready to be sliced. And this is one soufflé that won't let you down. You can leave it in a warm oven for up to half an hour before serving.

1 **pound broccoli**
6 **tablespoons butter or margarine**
¾ **cup all-purpose flour**
About 1 teaspoon dry mustard
About ½ teaspoon salt
3 **cups milk**
4 **eggs**
½ **cup milk**
1 **cup (4 oz.) shredded Cheddar or Longhorn cheese**

Cut broccoli into small flowerets and thinly slice stems. Steam over boiling water just until crisp-tender (4 to 6 minutes). Chop broccoli and set aside.

Preheat oven to 325°. Line the bottom of a greased jelly roll pan with foil; grease and lightly flour foil and set pan aside.

Melt butter in a 3-quart pan over medium heat. Stir in the ¾ cup flour, 1 teaspoon of the mustard, and ½ teaspoon of the salt. Cook, stirring, until flour is bubbly. Gradually pour in the 3 cups milk and continue cooking and stirring until sauce is smooth and thickened (8 to 10 minutes). Measure out 1 cup of this sauce and set aside.

Separate eggs. Beat yolks lightly and gradually beat in all but the 1 cup reserved sauce. Beat egg whites until short, stiff, moist peaks form; fold into egg yolk mixture. Pour into prepared pan. Bake in the preheated 325° oven for 35 to 40 minutes or until soufflé is golden brown and center springs back when lightly touched.

Meanwhile, in a pan over medium heat, combine the 1 cup reserved sauce and the ½ cup milk. Stir in cheese and cook, stirring, until cheese is melted. Sprinkle with more mustard and salt, if desired. Measure out 1 cup of the cheese sauce and combine with chopped broccoli.

When soufflé is done, immediately invert onto a clean towel. Starting at one narrow end, spread broccoli mixture over three-fourths of the soufflé. Using towel for support, roll up soufflé to enclose filling; place, seam side down, on a serving platter. (If not served at once, place in a 200° oven for as long as 30 minutes.) Reheat remaining cheese sauce over low heat, then pour over roll or serve individual slices and pour sauce over each. Makes 8 servings.

Per serving: 17 grams protein, 23 grams carbohydrate, 195 milligrams cholesterol, 368 calories.

Golden Cauliflower Quiche

Tender-crisp cauliflower, lots of Longhorn cheese, toasted almonds, and a creamy custard add up to a quiche with some delicious differences. Though you can use any pastry recipe for the 9-inch pie shell, we especially enjoy Oatmeal Pastry with this filling.

Oatmeal Pastry for a 9-inch deep-dish pie shell (page 87)

1 **small head (about 1 lb.) cauliflower**

½ **cup slivered almonds**

2 **eggs**

½ **cup *each* milk and mayonnaise**

2 **cups (8 oz.) shredded Longhorn cheese**

⅛ **teaspoon *each* pepper and ground nutmeg**

On a lightly floured board, roll out pastry about ⅛ inch thick. Fit into a deep 9-inch pie pan; crimp edge. Bake in a preheated 400° oven for 10 minutes. Let cool.

Meanwhile, break cauliflower into flowerets and cut into ½-inch-thick pieces. (You should have 4 cups.) Steam over boiling water until just crisp-tender (about 4 minutes). Drain, plunge into cold water to cool, then drain again.

Spread almonds in a shallow pan and toast in a 350° oven for about 8 minutes or until lightly browned. Place cauliflower in bottom of pastry shell and sprinkle with toasted almonds.

In a blender or food processor, whirl eggs, milk, and mayonnaise until smooth. Add 1¼ cups of the cheese, along with pepper and nutmeg, and whirl briefly to mix. Pour over cauliflower and nuts in pastry shell. Sprinkle with remaining ¾ cup cheese.

Bake on bottom rack of a 350° oven for 30 to 35 minutes or until a knife inserted in center comes out clean. Let stand on a wire rack for 10 minutes before serving. Makes 6 servings.

Per serving: 19 grams protein, 29 grams carbohydrate, 179 milligrams cholesterol, 586 calories.

Spinach & Feta Quiche

Spinach and feta cheese are often paired in Greek cooking and wrapped in flaky fila dough. Here they're cooked instead in a buttery whole wheat pastry shell. On a warm day, you may want to start your meal with chilled Make-ahead Gazpacho (page 35) and serve the quiche cooled, accompanied by a classic Greek salad or fresh fruit. For cooler weather, you can serve the quiche hot, with a cup of Potato Yogurt Soup (page 28).

Whole Wheat Pastry for a single crust 9-inch pie (page 87)

1 **package (10 oz.) frozen chopped spinach**

6 **ounces feta cheese, crumbled**

½ **cup cottage cheese**

6 **green onions (including tops), sliced**

1 **tablespoon olive oil**

1 **teaspoon dry basil**

½ **teaspoon pepper**

¼ **teaspoon garlic salt**

4 **eggs**

½ **cup milk**

Roll out pastry about ⅛ inch thick on a lightly floured board. Fit into a 9-inch pie pan; crimp edge. Bake in a preheated 400° oven for 10 minutes. Let cool.

Squeeze out as much liquid as possible from spinach; set aside. In a blender or food processor, whirl feta cheese, cottage cheese, onions, oil, basil, pepper, and garlic salt until smooth. Add eggs and milk and blend well. Add spinach and whirl briefly to mix. Pour into pastry shell.

Bake in a 400° oven for 20 minutes; reduce temperature to 350° and bake for 15 to 20 more minutes or until a knife inserted in center comes out clean. Let stand on a wire rack for 10 minutes or bring to room temperature before cutting into wedges to serve. Makes 6 servings.

Per serving: 18 grams protein, 31 grams carbohydrate, 245 milligrams cholesterol, 423 calories.

Mushroom-crust Quiche

Looking for a change-of-pace quiche? Try a change of crust. In this egg and cheese pie, mushrooms mixed with wheat germ and whole wheat bread crumbs take the place of the usual pastry crust. A simple butter lettuce salad makes a good accompaniment for a light supper.

> **5 tablespoons butter or margarine**
> **½ pound mushrooms, coarsely chopped**
> **⅓ cup fine dry whole wheat bread crumbs**
> **2 tablespoons wheat germ**
> **¾ cup (7 or 8) chopped green onions (including tops)**
> **2 cups (8 oz.) shredded Swiss or jack cheese**
> **1 cup cottage cheese**
> **3 eggs**
> **¼ teaspoon *each* thyme and marjoram leaves**
> **Paprika**

In a wide frying pan over medium heat, melt 3 tablespoons of the butter. Add mushrooms and cook until limp. Remove pan from heat and stir in bread crumbs and wheat germ. Turn into a well-greased 9-inch pie pan and press evenly onto bottom and sides.

In the same pan, melt the remaining 2 tablespoons butter. Add

onions and cook until soft. Spread onions over crust and sprinkle evenly with shredded cheese. In a blender or food processor, whirl cottage cheese, eggs, thyme, and marjoram until smooth. Pour into crust and sprinkle with paprika.

Bake in a 350° oven for 25 to 30 minutes or until a knife inserted in center comes out clean. Let stand on a wire rack for 10 minutes before serving. Makes 6 servings.

Per serving: 21 grams protein, 9 grams carbohydrate, 201 milligrams cholesterol, 345 calories.

Russian Quiche

Onion, mushrooms, Swiss cheese, yogurt, and a touch of horseradish make a tangy filling for this quiche. Sweet & Sour Borscht (page 33) would provide a tantalizing counterpoint of flavors. Or you can serve this substantial but not overly rich quiche with a beet or cucumber salad in dill-seasoned dressing.

> **9-inch unbaked pastry shell, 1½ inches deep**
> **1 tablespoon butter or margarine**
> **1 small onion, chopped**
> **¼ pound mushrooms, sliced**
> **½ teaspoon thyme leaves**
> **1 cup (4 oz.) shredded Swiss cheese**
> **3 eggs**
> **1 cup plain yogurt**
> **2 tablespoons all-purpose flour**
> **½ teaspoon prepared horseradish**
> **¼ teaspoon *each* salt and dry mustard**
> **Paprika**

Bake pastry shell in a preheated 450° oven for 7 to 10 minutes or until lightly browned. Let cool.

Meanwhile, melt butter in a wide frying pan over medium heat. Add onion and mushrooms and cook until onion is soft. Stir in thyme and let cool.

Sprinkle cheese evenly into pastry shell. Spoon onion mixture into shell. Beat eggs slightly, then stir in yogurt, flour, horseradish, salt, and mustard until well blended. Pour over mushroom layer. Sprinkle with paprika.

Bake in a 375° oven for 40 to 45 minutes or until filling is puffed and browned and a knife inserted in center comes out clean. Let stand on a wire rack for 10 minutes before serving. Makes 6 servings.

Per serving: 12 grams protein, 34 grams carbohydrate, 159 milligrams cholesterol, 320 calories.

Creamy Eggs & Sweet Onions

Slowly sautéed in butter, the onion slices in this creamy egg dish take on a golden hue and mellow sweetness. For a simple meal— similar to those enjoyed in French country homes—serve the eggs with crusty bread and fried potatoes, followed by a crisp green salad and fruit.

> **1¼ pounds small boiling onions**
> **2 tablespoons butter or margarine**
> **6 hard-cooked eggs**
> **¼ cup all-purpose flour**
> **2 cups milk**
> **Salt and pepper**

Cut onions in half through stem, then thinly slice. Melt butter in a heavy 3-quart pan over medium heat. Add onions and cook, stirring frequently, until soft but not browned (about 25 minutes).

Meanwhile, cut eggs into ½-inch-thick slices; set aside.

When onions are soft, gradually sprinkle in flour, stirring to mix well. Slowly pour in milk and cook, stirring, until sauce boils and thickens. Add salt and pepper to taste. Gently stir in all but 4 or 5 egg slices and cook until heated through. Garnish with reserved egg slices before serving. Makes 4 servings.

Per serving: 17 grams protein, 26 grams carbohydrate, 414 milligrams cholesterol, 338 calories.

Meringue-topped Vegetable Custard

Surprise! Lemon pie doesn't have a monopoly on meringue. For this savory vegetable custard dish, you make a meringue topping with grated Cheddar cheese folded into beaten egg whites. The topping, sprinkled lightly with sesame seeds, bakes to an appealing golden hue and forms an airy "crust" over the mixed vegetables beneath.

2 tablespoons butter or margarine

6 medium-size (2 lbs. total) zucchini, shredded

1 large green pepper, seeded and chopped

1 large onion, chopped

1 teaspoon *each* **salt and dry basil**

¼ teaspoon *each* **ground nutmeg and pepper**

2 tablespoons all-purpose flour

½ pint (1 cup) sour cream

6 eggs, separated

4 cups (1 lb.) shredded Cheddar cheese

2 tablespoons sesame seeds

Melt butter in a wide frying pan over medium-high heat. Add zucchini, green pepper, onion, salt, basil, nutmeg, and pepper. Cook, stirring often, until liquid evaporates (about 12 minutes). Add flour and cook for 1 minute. Let cool.

Beat together sour cream and egg yolks. Stir in vegetable mixture and 2 cups of the cheese. Spread in a well-buttered shallow 2-quart casserole. Beat egg whites until stiff, moist peaks form. Fold in remaining 2 cups cheese and spread over vegetable-custard mixture. Sprinkle with sesame seeds.

Bake in a 350° oven for about 55 minutes or until a knife inserted in center comes out clean. Let stand for 10 minutes before serving. Makes 8 servings.

Per serving: 23 grams protein, 12 grams carbohydrate, 243 milligrams cholesterol, 428 calories.

Fila Cheese Squares

Food for Greek gods! You make this version of Greek pie—called *borek*—by spreading layers of fila dough with a seasoned mixture of feta and ricotta cheeses. You bake it to a buttery gold color, let it cool slightly, then cut it into squares. It makes a marvelous meal accompanied by a platter of Vegetables à la Grecque (page 16). For an Olympian feast, include Stuffed Grape Leaves (page 59) too.

1 cup ricotta cheese

8 ounces feta cheese, crumbled

1 small package (3 oz.) cream cheese, softened

2 tablespoons all-purpose flour

2 eggs

½ teaspoon ground nutmeg

¼ teaspoon white pepper

½ cup chopped parsley

9 to 12 sheets (about ½ lb.) fila dough, each about 16 by 24 inches

½ cup butter, melted

With an electric mixer, beat ricotta, feta, and cream cheese with flour, eggs, nutmeg, and pepper until well blended. Stir in parsley.

Cut fila in half crosswise, then cover loosely to keep from drying out. With a pastry brush, coat bottom of a 9 by 13-inch baking pan with butter. Line pan with a sheet of fila. Brush fila lightly in a few places with melted butter. Cover with another sheet of fila and brush lightly with butter. Repeat until you have used half the fila.

Spread cheese mixture evenly over fila. Cover with another sheet of fila and brush lightly with butter; repeat with remaining fila. Brush top with remaining butter. (At this point, you may cover and refrigerate until next day.)

Just before baking, score top layer of fila with a sharp knife, marking off serving-size pieces: 2½ by 3-inch rectangles for entrée servings, or smaller pieces for appetizers.

Bake, uncovered, in a 375° oven for 35 minutes or until top of pastry is golden and crisp. Makes 15 entrée servings.

Per entrée serving: 6 grams protein, 10 grams carbohydrate, 60 milligrams cholesterol, 140 calories.

Fettuccine with Four Cheeses

Fontina, Bel Paese, and Gorgonzola blend to make a divine cheese sauce for this classic Italian dish. Parmesan, the fourth cheese, is tossed with the noodles and also passed around the table. All you need to complete a light meal is a crisp salad or vegetable vinaigrette. For dessert, serve a piquant Italian ice or fresh fruit.

3 tablespoons butter or margarine

1½ tablespoons all-purpose flour

⅛ teaspoon ground nutmeg Dash of white pepper

1 cup half-and-half (light cream)

½ cup vegetable stock (page 25)

⅓ cup *each* **shredded fontina and Bel Paese cheeses**

⅓ cup crumbled Gorgonzola cheese

8 ounces medium-wide noodles

¾ cup grated Parmesan cheese

(Continued on next page)

In a 2-quart pan over medium heat, melt 1½ tablespoons of the butter. Mix in flour, nutmeg, and pepper; cook, stirring, until bubbly. Slowly stir in half-and-half and stock; cook, stirring constantly, until sauce boils and thickens. Mix in fontina and Bel Paese cheeses; cook, stirring, until cheeses are melted and sauce is smooth. Stir in Gorgonzola cheese until blended; place pan over simmering water to keep sauce warm.

Cook noodles according to package directions. Drain well. Toss noodles lightly with remaining 1½ tablespoons butter and ½ cup of the Parmesan cheese. Spoon noodles onto serving plates. Top each serving with an equal amount of hot cheese sauce and the remaining ¼ cup Parmesan cheese. Makes 4 servings.

Per serving: 24 grams protein, 48 grams carbohydrate, 152 milligrams cholesterol, 584 calories.

Vegetarian Joe

A garden of vegetables goes into this variation of Joe's Special. Eggs and tofu provide the protein. It's delicious served with whole wheat toast or muffins.

½ **pound Italian green beans *or* 1 package (9 oz.) frozen Italian green beans, thawed**

1 **cup sliced cauliflower**

1 **package (10 oz.) frozen chopped spinach, thawed**

About 8 ounces tofu

1 **tablespoon *each* olive oil and butter**

1 **medium-size onion, chopped**

2 **cloves garlic, minced or pressed**

¼ **pound mushrooms, sliced**

½ **teaspoon *each* dry basil and oregano leaves**

½ **teaspoon *each* salt and vegetable-flavored granules**

6 **eggs**

½ **cup grated Parmesan cheese**

Remove ends and strings from beans; cut into 1½-inch lengths. Steam fresh beans and cauliflower over boiling water until crisp-tender (4 to 5 minutes). If using frozen beans, just drain well; do not cook. Squeeze spinach to remove excess moisture. Drain tofu, pat dry with paper towels, and cut into ¾-inch cubes.

Heat oil and butter in a wide frying pan over medium-high heat. Add onion, garlic, and mushrooms; cook, stirring occasionally, until onion is soft. Add beans, cauliflower, spinach, basil, oregano, salt, and granules. Reduce heat to medium-low and cook until heated through.

Beat eggs until blended; pour over vegetable mixture. Add tofu. Cook, gently lifting cooked portion to allow uncooked egg to flow underneath; cook until eggs are softly set. Sprinkle Parmesan cheese over individual servings. Makes 6 servings.

Per serving: 16 grams protein, 11 grams carbohydrate, 268 milligrams cholesterol, 228 calories.

Filled Oven Pancake

Oven pancakes—often called Dutch Babies—are usually baked until puffy around the edges. Then they're filled. In this version, though, you first cook the mushroom-and-onion filling in an ovenproof frying pan, then pour the pancake batter over the filling. The result is a generous puffy entrée that you can serve hot, right from the oven, for brunch or dinner. A chewy whole wheat bread and fruit salad would make perfect accompaniments.

About 5 tablespoons butter or margarine

½ **pound mushrooms, sliced**

1 **small onion, chopped**

1 **teaspoon dry basil**

¾ **teaspoon salt**

¼ **teaspoon *each* pepper and ground nutmeg**

4 **eggs**

1 **cup *each* milk and all-purpose flour**

⅓ **cup grated Parmesan cheese**

About ½ cup sour cream

¼ **cup thinly sliced green onions (including tops)**

In a 10 or 11-inch frying pan with an ovenproof handle, melt 3 tablespoons of the butter. Add mushrooms and onion and cook, stirring, until mushrooms are lightly browned. Stir in basil, salt, pepper, and nutmeg. Tip pan to estimate drippings, then add enough butter to make about 5 tablespoons fat.

In a blender or food processor, whirl eggs for 1 minute. With motor running, gradually pour in milk, then slowly add flour; whirl for 30 seconds. (Or, with a rotary beater, beat eggs until light; gradually beat in milk, then flour.)

Place pan with mushroom mixture in a 425° oven until pan is hot and butter is melted and bubbly. Remove pan from oven. Quickly pour in batter, sprinkle with cheese, and return to oven. Bake for 20 to 25 minutes or until puffy and browned. Top with sour cream and sprinkle with green onions. Serve immediately. Makes 4 servings.

Per serving: 23 grams protein, 37 grams carbohydrate, 340 milligrams cholesterol, 545 calories.

Corn Chili Strata

You build up a strata in layers: in this case, a layer of whole wheat bread, a layer of corn, a layer of zucchini, and a layer of chilies and jack cheese. Then you pour a custard mixture over the top and refrigerate the strata until the next day, if you like. The result is a custardy vegetable casserole sure to become a family favorite. It's also an excellent dish to serve buffet style or take to a potluck.

6 slices whole wheat bread
1 to 1½ tablespoons butter or margarine, softened
1 can (1 lb.) whole kernel corn, drained
2 cups thinly sliced zucchini or crookneck squash
1 can (4 oz.) diced green chili peppers
2 cups (8 oz.) shredded jack, Longhorn, or mild Cheddar cheese
4 eggs
2 cups milk
½ teaspoon salt
⅛ teaspoon pepper

Trim crusts from bread. Lightly spread slices with butter and fit into a lightly buttered 7 by 11-inch baking dish. Distribute corn in an even layer over bread, then arrange zucchini evenly over corn. Sprinkle chilies and cheese evenly over zucchini.

Beat eggs lightly, then beat in milk, salt, and pepper. Pour egg mixture over cheese. Cover and refrigerate for at least 4 hours or overnight.

Bake, uncovered, in a 375° oven for 30 to 40 minutes or until lightly browned and puffed; a knife inserted in center should come out clean. Let stand for 10 minutes before cutting into squares to serve. Makes 6 servings.

Per serving: 21 grams protein, 26 grams carbohydrate, 244 milligrams cholesterol, 372 calories.

Zesty Tomato Fondue

"Dive in!" That's the way to introduce this Italian-style fondue to your family and friends. It's a dish that's fun to serve any time, even at a small dinner party or out camping.

For diving in, we suggest dunking cubes of crusty French or sourdough bread, and dipping cooked artichoke leaves, lightly steamed whole baby carrots, green beans, broccoli, and cauliflower. For meat-eaters, you can offer oven-browned meatballs or pieces of cooked Italian sausages.

2 tablespoons butter or margarine
1 medium-size onion, finely chopped
1 clove garlic, minced or pressed
1 small can (about 8 oz.) stewed tomatoes
½ teaspoon dry basil
¼ teaspoon oregano leaves
⅛ teaspoon pepper
2 cups (8 oz.) shredded Longhorn cheese
¼ cup grated Parmesan cheese
1 tablespoon cornstarch

Melt butter in a 2-quart pan over medium heat. Cook onion and garlic, stirring occasionally, until

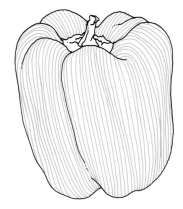

golden. Add tomatoes (break up with a spoon), basil, oregano, and pepper. Heat to simmering. Meanwhile, combine Longhorn and Parmesan cheeses with cornstarch.

Reduce heat to low and add cheese mixture, a handful at a time, stirring until cheeses are melted and blended. Transfer to fondue pot or chafing dish and keep warm over heat source. Serve with bread and vegetables for dipping. Makes 4 servings.

Per serving: 18 grams protein, 10 grams carbohydrate, 80 milligrams cholesterol, 337 calories.

Baked Brie

(Pictured on page 39)

Baked Brie is similar to *beignet au fromage* (deep-fried cheese), only simpler to prepare. You can use these same directions for a larger Brie to serve more people. Precede this elegant entrée with Tarragon Vegetable Salad (page 17) or Vegetables à la Grecque (page 16). Spread the hot Brie on slices of French bread, accompanied by grapes and sliced pears or apples. Then, with white wine, toast *bon appetit* to your friends.

2 tablespoons butter, softened
About 7 ounces whole ripe Brie or Camembert cheese with rind
2 tablespoons sliced almonds

Preheat oven to 350°.

Spread butter over top and sides of cheese. Place cheese on an ovenproof rimmed serving plate. Sprinkle almonds over top.

Bake in the preheated 350° oven for 12 to 15 minutes or until cheese just begins to melt. Makes 3 servings.

Per serving: 11 grams protein, 1 gram carbohydrate, 67 milligrams cholesterol, 240 calories.

Tangy, fresh flavor is the special bonus of making your own cheese and yogurt. Homemade cheese is marvelously light, delicate, and creamy. Homemade yogurt is thick, tangy, and velvety, far surpassing anything you've ever tasted from a carton. And besides tasting heavenly, both these foods are strong sources of protein.

Making cheese and yogurt is really quite simple. The only special equipment you'll need is a thermometer that will measure 170° to 175°F for cheese and 100° to 120°F for yogurt; a variety of such thermometers are available in cookware departments.

Making & Serving Cream Cheese

Kept refrigerated, this homemade cheese stays fresh for about a week. If you make more than you can use in that time, you can freeze the remainder. When you're ready to use it, let it thaw completely, then beat with an electric mixer.

Serve the cheese with fruit, or spread it on warm English muffins, toasted bagels, or sliced nut bread. Season it with herbs for an appetizer dip, or make it into one of the two desserts that follow the basic recipe.

Fresh Cream Cheese. In a heavy 6 to 8-quart kettle, combine 4 quarts **whole milk** and 1 quart **cultured buttermilk.** Attach a thermometer inside the kettle and place kettle over medium to medium-high heat; stir occasionally to prevent scorching. Too-frequent stirring breaks up the curds almost as fast as they form; you should stir gently, only every 5 to 10 minutes.

When the temperature reaches 170°, reduce heat to low and keep temperature between 170° and 175°.

Meanwhile, line a colander with 3 or 4 thicknesses of cheesecloth wrung out in cold water. Set colander inside a bowl beside the kettle of milk. When thick white curds separate from the watery whey, use a slotted spoon to scoop the curds into the colander.

When most of the curds have been removed, pour remaining curds and whey into colander. (Reserve whey—which contains some vitamins and protein—for making bread or soup, if you

wish.) Allow curds to drain for 2 to 3 hours. Scrape them into a bowl and mix in **salt** to taste. For a supersmooth texture, whirl in a blender or food processor. Makes 4 cups or 2 pounds cheese.

Per ounce (2 tablespoons): 4 grams protein, 1 gram carbohydrate, 18 milligrams cholesterol, 57 calories.

Fresh Cheese Cheesecake. In a blender or food processor, place 2 **eggs,** 1 pound (2 cups) **fresh cream cheese,** 1 cup **sugar,** 1 teaspoon grated **lemon peel,** 3 tablespoons **lemon juice,** and ½ teaspoon *each* **vanilla** and **salt.** Whirl until very smooth.

Pour into a well-buttered 8-inch layer cake pan (one with a solid bottom) and set inside a baking pan. Pour ½ inch boiling water into baking pan. Bake in 325° oven until a knife inserted in center comes out clean (45 to 55 minutes).

Remove from water, cool slightly, then turn onto a serving plate. Serve at room temperature or chilled. If desired, garnish with fruit. Makes 8 servings.

Per serving: 12 grams protein, 40 grams carbohydrate, 99 milligrams cholesterol, 298 calories.

Mascarpone. In a bowl, beat until smooth: ½ pound (1 cup) **fresh cream cheese,** ¼ cup **powdered sugar,** 2 tablespoons **half-and-half** (light cream), and 2 tablespoons **orange-flavored liqueur** (or 1 tablespoon frozen orange juice concentrate, undiluted). Mound on a serving plate. Serve with fresh **apricot halves.** Makes 4 servings.

Per serving: 11 grams protein, 24 grams carbohydrate, 35 milligrams cholesterol, 233 calories.

Making & Serving Yogurt

Given a little patience and the right temperature, yogurt almost makes itself. Then, if you like, you can take the delicious, creamy result and move along to further adventures. You can drain it to make cheese, or you can blend it with flavorings to make an Indian *raita* to cool the palate alongside a curry or any other hot and spicy dish.

The important factor in making successful yogurt is keeping the milk culture at a fairly constant temperature (about 115°) until it thickens. Yogurt bacteria are killed by higher temperatures; below 90° they become inactive.

Today many commercial yogurt makers are available that provide the right amount of heat. Also a variety of home methods will keep the milk warm. Here are two reliable methods.

Electric frying pan method.   Use a bowl or several canning jars for the yogurt containers. Set containers inside a deep kettle, then set the kettle inside an electric frying pan or on an electric griddle.

To preheat this system, fill yogurt containers with warm water (about 115°), then set containers inside the kettle, and fill the kettle with 115° water. Place a thermometer in the water surrounding the yogurt containers and turn the appliance setting to warm (or whatever setting will keep the water at 115°).

Cover the kettle with a lid or, if the containers are large, with a tent of foil. You can also set a folded bath towel on top of the foil to help hold in heat. Let stand while you heat milk and add starter (directions follow).

When mixture is ready, remove yogurt containers, pour out their water, and replace with milk mixture; return containers to the kettle. The yogurt will develop the most even consistency if the surrounding water is the same level as the yogurt inside the containers.

Leave containers undisturbed until yogurt has set (3½ to 5 hours). If water temperature should go as high as 120°, ladle out some of the water from the kettle, replace with cold water, and lower heat setting as needed. Refrigerate yogurt until cold and firm.

Vacuum bottle method.   Preheat a 1 or 2-quart wide-mouth vacuum bottle by filling it with warm water (about 115°). Cap the bottle and let stand while you heat milk and add starter (directions follow). When mixture is ready, pour water out of container and immediately replace it with milk mixture. Replace cap tightly and leave undisturbed for about 4 hours. Check, and if yogurt has not set, recap and test again every ½ hour. When set, remove lid, loosely cover, and refrigerate.

Thick Homemade Yogurt.   Pour 2 cups **low-fat milk** into a pan and place over medium heat. Heat to scalding (185°). Remove from heat and cool; discard skin. Meanwhile combine 1¼ cups **water** and 1⅓ cups **instant nonfat dry milk** powder and stir until smooth. Add this to the cooling milk, then check its temperature.

As soon as the mixture cools to 115°, stir in ¼ cup **plain commercial yogurt** until smooth. Transfer mixture to preheated yogurt container. Keep warm as directed for the method you are using. When set, usually in 3½ to 5 hours, remove from heat and refrigerate, covered, until cold. After the first batch, you can use your own yogurt for a starter as long as it is fresh—not more than a week old. Makes 1 quart.

Per ½-cup serving: 7 grams protein, 10 grams carbohydrate, 8 milligrams cholesterol, 81 calories.

Yogurt Cheese.   Wring out a clean dishcloth or 3 or 4 thicknesses of cheesecloth (cut 20 inches square) in cold water. Line a colander with the cloth. Spoon in 1 quart **thick homemade yogurt.** Twist ends of cloth together to close. Place colander in your sink (or set in a larger bowl) and let drain at room temperature for 24 hours or until yogurt is consistency of cream cheese. Cover and refrigerate. Makes 1½ cups.

Per tablespoon: 1.3 grams protein, 2 grams carbohydrate, 3 milligrams cholesterol, 19 calories.

Mint & Coriander Raita (*pictured on page 63).*   In a bowl, combine 2 cups **plain yogurt,** ¼ cup chopped fresh **mint leaves,** ¼ cup chopped **red onion,** 2 tablespoons chopped fresh **coriander** (cilantro), 1 tablespoon minced canned **green chili pepper,** and **salt** to taste. Makes 8 servings.

Per serving: 2 grams protein, 4 grams carbohydrate, 4 milligrams cholesterol, 34 calories.

Cucumber & Tomato Raita (*pictured on page 63).*   In a bowl, combine 2 cups **plain yogurt;** 1 medium-size **cucumber,** peeled, seeded, and chopped; 1 large **tomato,** peeled and chopped; 1 teaspoon ground **cumin;** ½ teaspoon **paprika;** and **salt** to taste. Makes 8 servings.

Per serving: 2 grams protein, 4 grams carbohydrate, 4 milligrams cholesterol, 34 calories.

Greens, Grains & Other Good Entrées

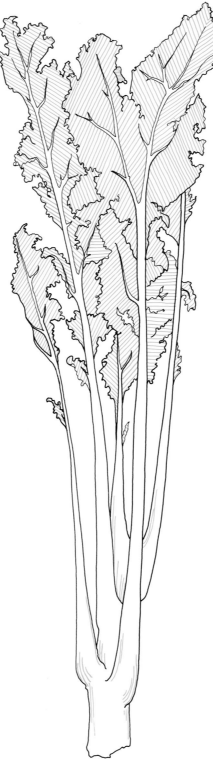

"What goes in that empty space on my plate where the meat used to be?"

A delicious entrée from this chapter, that's what! The question "Where's the meat?" won't even arise when you're serving such dishes as Eggplant Cannelloni (page 54) that uses slices of eggplant to enclose a savory cheese and mushroom filling. And you certainly won't hear it when you offer a meal-in-itself slice of Whole Wheat Zucchini Pizza (page 54), or a delicious Vegetable Kebab (page 57).

In fact, Vegetable Kebabs elicited this inquiry from one of our taste-test panelists: "What kind of meat is on the kebabs?" There wasn't any meat, of course. The well-seasoned, marinated chunks of grilled mushrooms and eggplant were simply satisfying replacements for meat.

Speaking of meat replacements, we haven't included any recipes for meat substitutes, sometimes called meat analogues—"burgers" made of processed soy, "meat loaves" made of nuts and beans. Our feeling is that if you're going vegetarian, you might as well enjoy the many virtues of grains, beans, and vegetables for themselves, rather than attempt to cook dishes that supposedly resemble meat in taste and texture.

That's why this chapter is a veritable kitchens-of-the-world tour. From Mexico's kitchen come the Green Enchiladas (page 51) and Chiles Rellenos Casserole (page 51), and you'll also recognize a south-of-the-border accent in Bulgur Mexicana (page 52) and Sonora Pizza (page 52). From Italy's kitchen comes inspiration for Lasagne Swirls (page 53) and Ricotta Gnocchi (page 53).

From India, we're pleased to include India-spiced Eggplant (page 62), Savory Fried Rice (page 64), and Vegetable Curry (page 62)—a royal feast, indeed. Traveling yet farther East, we bring back Sweet & Sour Soybeans (page 51), Savory Vegetables & Tofu (page 61), and Sesame Tofu Sticks (page 59).

Many of the dishes in this section need merely the addition of a simple green salad or perhaps a little soup and bread, with fruit for dessert, to make a complete meal. The Bulgur Mexicana and Eggplant Cannelloni, as well as Layered Chili (page 49), are in that category.

You'll find other entrées that need to share the spotlight. Sesame Tofu Sticks, for example, are excellent with steamed or stir-fried vegetables (pages 68 and 69); and the Armenian Vegetable Casserole (page 60), a Middle-eastern version of ratatouille, is best served over a pilaf of bulgur wheat or mixed grains. Another example is the Vegetable Kebabs, so delicious served with the exotic combination of dried apricots, dates, and rice known as Fruited Rice Pilaf (page 67).

Cooking Beans

Beans are about the best nutrition bargain going. Low in cost, they provide thiamin, riboflavin, niacin, iron, and calcium. When complemented by grains or dairy products, they're a main source of high-quality protein for vegetarians.

The simplest cooking directions are to sort through the beans and discard any bad ones, then rinse well, drain, and gently boil, uncovered, in three times their volume of water until tender.

For some beans, cooking "until tender" can take a considerable length of time. If you prefer, you can shorten their cooking time by soaking them according to one of the following methods.

Quick soaking. In a kettle, combine 6 to 8 cups **hot water** with 1 pound **dry beans**. Bring to a boil over high heat and continue to boil for 2 minutes. Remove from heat and let soak, covered, for 1 hour before draining.

Long soaking. In a kettle, combine 6 to 7 cups **cold water** with 1 pound **dry beans**. Add 2 teaspoons **salt**, (it helps beans absorb water evenly). Let soak for at least 3 to 4 hours or until next day. Drain before cooking.

To cook soaked beans. In a kettle, bring 6 to 7 cups water to a boil. Add drained, soaked beans. Boil gently, partially covered, until tender. (See list of legumes at right for cooking times.) Add water if needed to keep beans covered. Add salt to taste (up to 2 teaspoons) when beans are tender. Drain excess water when done; reserve for soups or stews, if desired.

Beans double in size; 1 pound dry beans yields about 4 cups cooked beans. We prefer to cook a large quantity of beans and freeze whatever we don't plan to use right away.

The following list of legumes (mostly beans) contains a brief description as well as recommended cooking time *after soaking* for each item. Note that lentils and split peas do not need soaking.

Black beans. Robust flavor; popular in South American cooking. 1 to 1½ hours.

Black-eyed peas. Smooth texture, pealike flavor; good mixed with other vegetables. 1 to 1½ hours.

Garbanzos (chick peas, ceci). Firm texture, nutlike flavor; naturals for minestrone, salads. 2 to 2½ hours.

Great Northern beans. Mild flavor; good in soups, and combined with other vegetables. 1 to 1½ hours.

Kidney beans. Firm texture, meaty flavor; hold shape well in chili dishes and other casseroles. 1½ to 2 hours.

Lentils. No soaking needed. Mild flavor blends well with many different foods, spices. 40 to 45 minutes.

Limas, baby. Versatile; use like other white beans in soups, casseroles. 1 to 1½ hours.

Pink, pinto, and red beans. Hearty flavor; great for barbecue-style beans, Mexican cooking, soups, casseroles. 1½ to 2 hours.

Soybeans. Strong-flavored, near-perfect protein source. Refrigerate while soaking. 3 to 3½ hours.

Split peas, green and yellow. No soaking; good for soups, side dishes. 40 to 45 minutes.

White beans (navy), small. Hold their shape when cooked; classic for baked beans. 1 to 1½ hours.

Layered Chili

(Pictured on page 50)

This is no timid chili. It's liberally spiced without being too hot. To serve, you pass special pink onions, cheese, and a variety of toppings to layer on each steaming bowl. As a shortcut, you can use canned kidney beans.

4 large onions, chopped
1 large green pepper, seeded and chopped
3 tablespoons salad oil
1 tablespoon *each* mustard seeds and chili powder
1 teaspoon *each* cumin seeds and unsweetened cocoa
¼ teaspoon ground cinnamon
1 can (about 1 lb.) tomatoes
5 cups cooked kidney beans plus 1½ cups cooking liquid or water, or 3 cans (about 1 lb. size) kidney beans, undrained, and 1 cup water
1 can (6 oz.) tomato paste
Salt
Pink Onions (recipe follows)
Relish toppings (suggestions follow)
2 limes or lemons, cut in wedges

In a 5 or 6-quart kettle, cook onions and green pepper in oil over medium high heat, stirring occasionally, until onions are golden and pepper is soft. Add mustard seeds and cook, stirring, for 1 minute. Add chili powder, cumin seeds, cocoa, cinnamon, tomatoes (break up with a spoon) and their liquid, beans and their liquid, and tomato paste. Reduce heat and simmer rapidly, uncovered, for about 40 minutes or until most of the liquid has cooked away and chili is thickened; stir frequently to prevent scorching.

Season with salt to taste (not necessary if using canned beans). Pass pink onions, relish toppings, and lime wedges to layer on top of chili. Makes 6 servings.

Per serving (including pink onions and relishes): 28 grams protein, 69 grams carbohydrate, 37 milligrams cholesterol, 563 calories.

Pink Onions. In a 1-quart pan over high heat, bring 2 cups **water** and 1½ tablespoons **vinegar** to a boil. Add 1 large **red onion** (thinly sliced) and push down into liquid. (Use white onion if red is not available, but it won't turn pink.) Return to a boil and cook, uncovered, over

(Continued on page 51)

...Layered Chili (cont'd.)
medium heat for 2 to 3 minutes. Drain onion and let cool. In a bowl, stir together onion, 1½ teaspoons **vinegar,** 1 tablespoon **salad oil,** ½ teaspoon **mustard seeds,** ¼ teaspoon **cumin seeds,** and **salt** to taste. Serve at room temperature, or cover and chill until ready to serve.

Relish toppings. Arrange in containers 3 medium-size **tomatoes** (chopped), 1 can (7 oz.) diced **green chilies,** 1 medium-size **cucumber** (peeled and chopped), 1 cup sliced **green onions** (including tops), and 2 cups (8 oz.) shredded **Cheddar cheese.**

Sweet & Sour Soybeans

Pineapple chunks and a bevy of fresh vegetables combine with soybeans in a pert sweet-sour sauce. It's delicious over rice.

 Sweet-Sour Sauce (recipe follows)
 2 tablespoons salad oil
 1 large onion, cut in 1-inch squares
 2 large carrots, cut in ¼-inch slices
 1 clove garlic, minced or pressed
 1 green pepper, seeded and cut into 1-inch squares
 ¾ cup fresh pineapple chunks, or canned pineapple chunks, drained
 2 tomatoes, cut in wedges
 2½ cups cooked soybeans (page 49)

Prepare sweet-sour sauce and reserve.

Ladle up a steaming bowl of Layered Chili (recipe on page 49). Then make it live up to its name—pile on layers of cheese and other condiments. A wedge of Quick Corn Bread (recipe on page 78) complements the chili and completes the protein.

Heat oil in a wide frying pan over high heat; add onion, carrots, and garlic and cook, stirring, for about 3 minutes or until vegetables are crisp-tender. Add green pepper and cook for 1 minute. Add pineapple, tomatoes, and soybeans and cook for 2 minutes or until hot. Stir sweet-sour sauce, pour into pan, and continue to cook, stirring, until sauce bubbles and thickens. Makes 6 servings.

Per serving: 10 grams protein, 72 grams carbohydrate, no cholesterol, 391 calories.

Sweet-Sour Sauce. In a bowl, combine 1½ tablespoons *each* **cornstarch, soy sauce,** and **dry sherry;** ½ cup *each* **brown sugar** and **wine vinegar;** and ⅓ cup **vegetable stock** (page 25).

Green Enchiladas

Spinach and green chilies in a creamy sauce account for the "green" in this recipe. The enchiladas themselves are corn tortillas wrapped around a mild cheese and onion filling.

 1 tablespoon salad oil
 2 large onions, chopped
 ¼ teaspoon salt
 Salad oil
 12 corn tortillas
 3 cups (12 oz.) shredded jack cheese
 1 package (10 oz.) frozen chopped spinach, thawed
 2 green onions (including tops), sliced
 1 can (4 oz.) diced green chili peppers
 1 can (10½ oz.) condensed cream of mushroom soup
 ½ pint (1 cup) sour cream

Heat the 1 tablespoon oil in a wide frying pan over medium heat. Add onions and cook until soft (about 5

minutes). Stir in salt; set pan aside.

In a small frying pan, heat a little oil over medium heat. One at a time, dip tortillas in oil for a few seconds on each side or just until soft; drain briefly. Across the middle of each tortilla, sprinkle 2 tablespoons *each* cooked onion and shredded cheese. Roll to enclose. Place tortillas, seam side down, in a greased shallow 9 by 13-inch baking pan.

Squeeze spinach to remove excess moisture. In a blender or food processor, purée spinach, green onions, chili peppers, soup, and sour cream until smooth. Pour sauce over tortillas. Sprinkle remaining cheese over all.

Bake, uncovered, in a 350° oven for 30 minutes or until hot and bubbly. Makes 12 enchiladas.

Per enchilada: 11 grams protein, 22 grams carbohydrate, 39 milligrams cholesterol, 273 calories.

Chiles Rellenos Casserole

Instead of stuffing and frying the chili peppers in true chiles rellenos fashion, you cover them with two kinds of cheese and bake them in a puffy batter. For a south-of-the-border dinner, serve the casserole with refried beans, warm tortillas, and a salad of greens, oranges, and red onions.

 2 cans (7 oz. *each*) whole green chili peppers
 3 cups (12 oz.) shredded sharp Cheddar cheese
 4 green onions (including tops), thinly sliced
 3 cups (12 oz.) shredded mozzarella cheese
 6 eggs
 3 cups milk
 ¾ cup all-purpose flour
 ¼ teaspoon salt
 2 cans (7 oz. *each*) green chili salsa

(Continued on next page)

Split chili peppers lengthwise and remove seeds and pith. Spread chilies in a single layer in a greased 9 by 13-inch baking dish. Sprinkle Cheddar cheese, green onions, and 1½ cups of the mozzarella cheese over chilies.

In a bowl, beat eggs, milk, flour, and salt together until smooth. Pour over chilies and cheese. Bake in a 325° oven for 50 minutes or until a knife inserted in custard comes out clean.

Meanwhile, mix salsa with the remaining 1½ cups mozzarella cheese. Sprinkle over casserole and return to oven for 10 minutes or until cheese melts. Let stand for 5 minutes before serving. Makes 10 servings.

Per serving: 32 grams protein, 21 grams carbohydrate, 268 milligrams cholesterol, 474 calories.

Sonora Pizza

This Mexican-flavored pizza has enough elements to make a great entrée: crisp-fried whole wheat tortillas, refried beans, cheese, chilies, crunchy vegetables, and a crown of sour cream. You assemble the base before you heat it in the oven. Then, if you wish, you can set out the condiments and let everyone be creative.

> Salad oil
> 8 large whole wheat tortillas (page 81)
> Spicy Tomato Sauce (recipe follows)
> 1 can (1 lb.) refried beans
> 1 can (4 oz.) *each* diced green chili peppers and chopped ripe olives
> 1 large onion, chopped
> 3 cups (12 oz.) shredded jack cheese or Cheddar cheese
> About 3 cups shredded lettuce
> About 1 cup thinly sliced radishes
> About ½ cup sour cream
> 1 cup alfalfa sprouts

Place a 10-inch frying pan over medium heat. Pour oil into pan to a depth of ½ inch and heat to 375° on a deep-frying thermometer. Fry one tortilla at a time, turning quickly several times with 2 wide spatulas, until bubbly and just golden (about 30 seconds total). Lift tortilla and let excess oil drain back into pan; drain on paper towels. If fried ahead, cool, package airtight in plastic bags, and store up to 2 days at room temperature.

Prepare spicy tomato sauce.

To assemble pizza, gently spread unheated beans in an even layer over each tortilla. Top each with about 2 tablespoons of the tomato sauce. Sprinkle chili peppers, olives, and onion over tortillas, then top with shredded cheese. Arrange on baking sheets.

Bake tortillas in a 350° oven until beans are hot and cheese is bubbly (7 to 10 minutes). Pass individual bowls of lettuce, radishes, sour cream, and alfalfa sprouts to be spooned over individual servings. Makes 8 servings.

Per serving: 20 grams protein, 41 grams carbohydrate, 69 milligrams cholesterol, 499 calories.

Spicy Tomato Sauce. In a pan over low heat, combine 1 can (15 oz.) **tomato sauce,** 2 cloves **garlic** (minced or pressed), 1½ teaspoons **chili powder,** and ½ teaspoon *each* **salt, oregano** leaves, and ground **cumin.** Simmer, uncovered, for 10 minutes.

Bulgur Mexicana

Here's a main-dish pilaf that's fast to prepare and fun to eat. The flavors will remind you of Spanish rice, and the dish is served like a tostada with a selection of condiments on top. Make-ahead Gazpacho (page 35) would be the perfect first course for this entrée.

> 2 tablespoons butter or margarine
> 1 medium-size onion, chopped
> 1 cup bulgur wheat
> 1 large stalk celery, thinly sliced
> ½ green or red bell pepper, seeded and diced
> 1 teaspoon chili powder
> ¾ teaspoon ground cumin
> 2¼ cups vegetable stock (page 25)
> Salt and pepper
> Condiments (suggestions follow)

Melt butter in a wide frying pan over medium heat. Add onion and bulgur and cook, stirring occasionally, until onion is soft and bulgur is golden (7 to 8 minutes). Stir in celery, bell pepper, chili powder, and cumin and cook for 2 minutes. Pour in stock and bring to a boil. Reduce heat to low; cover and simmer until all liquid is absorbed (about 20 minutes). Season to taste with salt and pepper.

To serve, mound bulgur mixture on a platter or individual plates. At the table, offer condiments, each in a separate bowl. Makes 4 servings.

Per serving (including condiments): 17 grams protein, 48 grams carbohydrate, 54 milligrams cholesterol, 469 calories.

Condiments. Prepare 1 cup *each* shredded **Cheddar cheese** and **alfalfa sprouts;** ⅓ cup *each* sliced **green onions** (including tops), **sunflower seeds,** and **sour cream;** 2 **tomatoes** (diced); and **bottled taco sauce.**

Lasagne Swirls

Here's meatless magic with pasta. Instead of layering wide lasagna noodles in a baking dish, you wrap them around a low fat, high protein ricotta cheese filling. The result is a platter of pinwheels that are as pretty as they are delicious.

- **16 packaged lasagne noodles**
  Boiling salted water
- **2 packages (10 oz. *each*) frozen chopped spinach, thawed**
- **2 cups (6 oz.) grated Parmesan cheese**
- **2⅔ cups ricotta cheese**
- **1 teaspoon *each* salt and pepper**
- **½ teaspoon ground nutmeg**
- **2 cloves garlic, minced or pressed**
- **1 large onion, chopped**
- **3 tablespoons olive oil or salad oil**
- **2 large cans (15 oz. *each*) tomato sauce**
- **¼ cup dry red wine**
- **½ teaspoon *each* dry basil and oregano leaves**

Cook noodles in a large kettle of boiling salted water according to package directions. Drain, rinse with cold water, and drain again.

Squeeze spinach to remove excess moisture. In a bowl, mix spinach with 1½ cups of the Parmesan cheese. Add ricotta, salt, ½ teaspoon of the pepper, and nutmeg; mix together. Spread about ¼ cup of this cheese mixture along entire length of each noodle; roll noodles up. Butter two 9 by 13-inch baking dishes. In each dish stand rolled noodles on end so they do not touch.

In a wide frying pan over medium heat, cook garlic and onion in olive oil until onion is soft. Add tomato sauce, wine, basil, oregano, and the remaining ½ teaspoon pepper. Simmer, uncovered, for 10 minutes. Pour sauce around noodles. If made ahead, cover and refrigerate.

Bake, covered, in a 350° oven for about 30 minutes (40 minutes, if refrigerated) or until heated through. Remove from oven and sprinkle lasagne evenly with remaining ½ cup Parmesan cheese. Makes 16 swirls.

Per swirl: 16 grams protein, 25 grams carbohydrate, 58 milligrams cholesterol, 281 calories.

Vegetable Lasagne

Your guests may never guess that this vegetable-laden lasagne is meatless. Cheese supplies a good deal of the protein, and you can add more by using whole wheat noodles.

- **⅓ cup olive oil or salad oil**
- **1 large onion, chopped**
- **2 cloves garlic, minced or pressed**
- **1 medium-size unpeeled eggplant (about 1 lb.), diced**
- **¼ pound mushrooms, sliced**
- **1 can (about 1 lb.) Italian-style tomatoes**
- **1 can (8 oz.) tomato sauce**
- **½ cup dry red wine**
- **1 medium-size carrot, shredded**
- **¼ cup chopped parsley**
- **2 teaspoons oregano leaves**
- **1 teaspoon *each* dry basil and salt**
- **¼ teaspoon pepper**
- **16 packaged whole wheat or regular lasagne noodles**
  Boiling salted water
- **2 cups (1 lb.) ricotta cheese**
- **2 cups (8 oz.) shredded mozzarella cheese**
- **1½ cups (4½ oz.) grated Parmesan cheese**

Heat oil in a wide frying pan over medium heat. Add onion, garlic, eggplant, and mushrooms and cook, stirring frequently, for 15

minutes. Add tomatoes and their liquid (break up tomatoes with a spoon), tomato sauce, wine, carrot, parsley, oregano, basil, salt, and pepper. Bring to a boil, then reduce heat and simmer, covered, for 30 minutes. Uncover and continue cooking until sauce is thick. You should have 5 cups sauce; set aside.

Cook noodles in a large kettle of boiling salted water according to package directions. Drain, rinse with cold water, and drain again.

Butter a 9 by 13-inch baking dish. Spread about ¼ of the sauce in dish. Arrange ⅓ of the noodles in an even layer over sauce. Dot noodles with ⅓ of the ricotta. Sprinkle with ⅓ of the mozzarella, then with ¼ of the Parmesan cheese. Repeat this layering two more times. Spread remaining sauce evenly over top and sprinkle with remaining Parmesan cheese. If made ahead, cover and refrigerate.

Bake, uncovered, in a 350° oven until hot and bubbly (40 to 50 minutes). Cut in squares to serve. Makes 10 servings

Per serving (made with whole wheat noodles): 26 grams protein, 44 grams carbohydrate, 20 milligrams cholesterol, 504 calories.

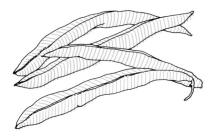

Ricotta Gnocchi

Think of these ricotta dumplings as vegetarian meatballs. They're firm, but tender and delicious. Serve them with tomato sauce on spaghetti, rice, or polenta (cooked cornmeal). If you prepare them ahead, or have any left over, reheat by steaming over boiling water for 5 minutes or by browning in butter.

(Continued on next page)

Fresh Tomato Sauce (recipe
follows)
1 egg
1 cup (8 oz.) ricotta cheese
½ cup fine dry bread crumbs
¾ cup grated Parmesan cheese
¼ teaspoon garlic salt
Dash of pepper
⅛ teaspoon ground nutmeg
½ teaspoon dry basil
1 package (10 oz.) frozen
chopped spinach, thawed
All-purpose flour
Boiling salted water

Prepare fresh tomato sauce.

In a large bowl, beat egg. Add
ricotta and mix well. Stir in bread
crumbs, ½ cup of the Parmesan,
garlic salt, pepper, nutmeg, and
basil. Squeeze spinach to remove
excess moisture. Stir spinach into
ricotta mixture. Shape mixture into
1½-inch balls. Roll in flour to coat
lightly.

Drop balls gently into a large kettle of boiling salted water. When
water returns to a boil, adjust heat
so water boils *very* gently. Cook for
10 minutes. Meanwhile, reheat
fresh tomato sauce. Remove balls
with a slotted spoon, drain well,
and place in a serving dish. Pour
tomato sauce over gnocchi;
sprinkle with the remaining ¼ cup
Parmesan. Makes 4 servings.

*Per serving (including fresh tomato
sauce):* 20 grams protein, 22 grams
carbohydrate, 113 milligrams cholesterol, 322 calories.

Fresh Tomato Sauce.   In a
2-quart pan over medium heat,
melt 1½ tablespoons **butter** or
margarine. Add 1 medium-size
onion (chopped) and cook until
soft. Add 2 large **tomatoes** (peeled
and finely chopped), 1 cup **vegetable stock** (page 25), ½ teaspoon
dry **basil** , ¼ teaspoon **salt** and a
dash of **pepper.** Bring to a boil
over high heat and cook for 10
minutes, stirring frequently; then
reduce heat to medium and continue to cook, stirring occasionally,
until sauce has thickened.

Whole Wheat Zucchini Pizza

(Pictured on facing page)

First you prepare a chewy whole
wheat crust topped with an amply
spiced tomato sauce. Then you
pile up the goodies—artichoke
hearts, cheese, zucchini, olives,
and on and on.

1 package active dry yeast
1½ cups warm water (about 110°)
2 tablespoons salad oil
1 teaspoon *each* salt, sugar, dry
basil, and oregano leaves
¼ cup wheat germ
1½ cups *each* all-purpose flour
and whole wheat flour
All-purpose flour for kneading
Tomato Sauce (recipe
follows)
2 medium-size zucchini, thinly
sliced
½ green or red bell pepper,
seeded and thinly sliced
4 green onions (including tops),
thinly sliced
1 can (2¼ oz.) sliced ripe olives
1 can (14 oz.) artichoke hearts,
drained and quartered
3 cups (12 oz.) shredded jack
cheese
¼ cup grated Parmesan cheese

In a large bowl, dissolve yeast in
water. Add oil, salt, sugar, basil,
oregano, wheat germ, and all-
purpose flour. Beat until smooth
(about 3 minutes, if using electric
mixer). Using a heavy-duty mixer
or wooden spoon, beat in whole
wheat flour until dough holds
together.

Turn out onto a lightly floured
board and knead until dough is
smooth and elastic (about 5 minutes). Turn over in a greased bowl,
cover, and let rise in a warm place
until dough has doubled in size
(about 45 minutes). Meanwhile,
prepare tomato sauce.

Punch dough down and divide in
half. Roll out each half to form a
14-inch circle, then transfer each

circle onto a greased 14-inch pizza
pan. One at a time, bake on next-
to-bottom rack of a 450° oven for
about 7 minutes or just until bottom of crust starts to brown. During
baking, watch carefully and prick
any bubbles that form. Remove
from oven and set aside.

To assemble pizza, spread
tomato sauce over crust. Arrange
zucchini, bell pepper, green
onions, olives, and artichoke quarters over sauce. Sprinkle jack
cheese and Parmesan over all.

Bake in a 450° oven for 12 to
15 minutes or until cheese melts.
Cut hot pizzas in wedges to serve.
Makes 2 pizzas; each serves 6.

Per serving: 22 grams protein, 50
grams carbohydrate, 44 milligrams
cholesterol, 464 calories.

Tomato Sauce.   In a wide frying
pan over medium heat, cook 1
large **onion** (chopped) in 2 tablespoons **olive oil** or salad oil until
soft. Stir in 1 can (15 oz.) **tomato
sauce,** 1 can (6 oz.) **tomato paste,**
½ cup **red wine,** 1 teaspoon *each*
oregano leaves and dry **basil,** and
½ teaspoon **salt.** Simmer, uncovered, for 10 minutes.

Eggplant Cannelloni

Thin, browned slices of eggplant
replace the usual pasta or crêpe
wrapping in this light but luscious
dish. To complete the meal, serve a
whole-grain pilaf and a green
salad.

(Continued on page 56)

*Supper in a single slice— Whole Wheat
Zucchini Pizza (recipe on this page)
has it all—a chewy crust, rich tomato
sauce with a double order of cheeses,
then vegetables galore.*

...Eggplant Cannelloni (cont'd.)

1 large (about 1½ lbs.)
eggplant

1 egg

⅔ cup milk

3 tablespoons salad oil

¼ cup whole wheat flour

1¼ cups (5 oz.) shredded jack
cheese

½ cup ricotta cheese

¾ cup grated Parmesan cheese

⅔ cup coarsely chopped fresh
mushrooms

2 eggs, lightly beaten

2 tablespoons chopped parsley

⅛ teaspoon *each* salt and
pepper
Fresh Tomato Sauce (page 54)

Remove stem from eggplant. Cut unpeeled eggplant lengthwise in slices ¼ inch thick. You should have 12 large slices; save small pieces for another use.

In a pie pan, beat until smooth the 1 egg, milk, 1 tablespoon of the oil, and flour. Place a wide frying pan on medium heat and add 1 tablespoon of the oil. Or set an electric griddle at 350° and add oil as needed. One at a time, dip eggplant slices in batter and drain briefly. Place slices in a single layer in pan and cook for about 10 minutes on each side or until lightly browned and very soft when pressed. Adding more oil as needed, repeat until all eggplant is cooked.

In a bowl, combine jack and ricotta cheeses, ½ cup of the Parmesan, mushrooms, the 2 eggs, parsley, salt, and pepper. Divide mixture into 12 equal portions. Spoon 1 portion across center of each eggplant slice; fold narrow end of slice over filling and roll to enclose. Arrange eggplant cannelloni, seam side down, in a single layer in a shallow 3-quart casserole. If made ahead, cover and refrigerate until next day.

Prepare fresh tomato sauce. Just before baking, spoon sauce over eggplant. Bake, uncovered, in a 375° oven for 15 to 20 minutes (25 minutes, if refrigerated) or until hot throughout.

To serve, sprinkle with the remaining ¼ cup Parmesan cheese. Makes 6 servings.

Per serving (including sauce): 19 grams protein, 16 grams carbohydrate, 181 milligrams cholesterol, 372 calories.

Whole Wheat Crêpes

Tender crêpes with their rich, whole wheat flavor make fine wrappers for sweet or savory fillings. Be sure you let the batter sit for at least an hour before cooking the crêpes so the bran in the whole wheat flour has a chance to soften.

With a batch of these made ahead and stored in the freezer, you have the handy starting point for a variety of entrées.

3 eggs

1 cup milk

⅔ cup whole wheat flour
About 4 teaspoons butter or
margarine

In a blender or food processor (or with a wire whip or electric mixer), blend eggs and milk; add flour and blend until smooth. Let stand at room temperature for 1 hour.

Place a 6 or 7-inch crêpe pan or other flat-bottomed frying pan over medium heat. When hot, add ¼ teaspoon of the butter and swirl to coat surface. Stir batter and pour about 2 tablespoons (all at once) into hot pan; immediately lift and tilt pan so batter covers entire bottom of pan. (Don't worry if there are a few little holes.) Return to heat and cook until surface appears dry and edge is lightly browned. With a spatula, turn and brown other side. Turn out onto a plate, stacking crêpes as made. If made ahead, cool, then place wax paper between each crêpe; package airtight (in quantities you expect to use) and refrigerate for as long as 3 days or freeze for longer storage. Allow crêpes to

come to room temperature before separating; they tear if cold. Fill crêpes as desired and roll or fold to enclose. Makes about 16 crêpes.

Per crêpe: 2 grams protein, 4 grams carbohydrate, 58 milligrams cholesterol, 67 calories.

Potato-Onion Blintzes

(Pictured on page 31)

For these savory blintzes, you enclose mashed potatoes and onions in whole wheat crêpes. The little packets, browned in butter, can be topped with sour cream or yogurt and your choice of poppy, sesame, sunflower, or pumpkin seeds. Potato-Onion Blintzes are the natural companions for Sweet & Sour Borscht (page 33).

About 16 whole wheat crêpes
(recipe at left)

2 tablespoons butter or
margarine

1 large onion, finely chopped

2 cups mashed, unseasoned
potatoes (3 medium-size
potatoes)

1 egg

½ teaspoon salt
White pepper
About 4 tablespoons butter
or margarine
About 1 cup sour cream or
plain yogurt
Finely chopped chives or
green onion
Poppy seeds, sesame seeds,
sunflower seeds, or pumpkin
seeds

Prepare crêpes.

In a small frying pan over medium heat, melt butter. Add onion and cook, stirring occasionally, until golden brown (about 15 minutes). Stir into mashed potatoes. Beat egg and stir into potatoes along with salt and a dash of pepper.

For each blintz, place a crêpe,

browned side up, on a flat surface. Spoon about 2 tablespoons of the potato mixture onto center of crêpe. Fold opposite sides over center so they overlap slightly, then fold bottom up over sides and roll over top to enclose. Place, folded side down, on a pan or tray. Repeat until all crêpes are filled. If made ahead, cover and refrigerate until next day.

Before serving, melt 2 tablespoons of the butter in a wide frying pan over medium heat. Place blintzes, folded sides down, in pan. Cook, turning carefully, until both sides are browned. Add more butter, about 1 tablespoon at a time, as needed, and brown remaining blintzes. Keep warm in a low oven until all are cooked. Serve hot with sour cream, chives, and your choice of seeds. Makes 16 blintzes.

Per blintz: 4 grams protein, 5 grams carbohydrate, 26 milligrams cholesterol, 111 calories.

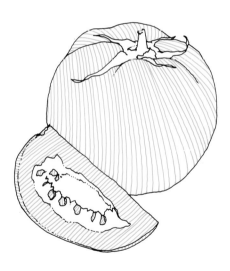

Mushroom-Broccoli Stroganoff

Spinach noodles and fresh vegetables team up for a family-pleasing casserole. Sour cream and two kinds of cheese give this entrée its tangy richness.

2 **tablespoons butter or margarine**
1 **large onion, chopped**
½ **pound mushrooms, sliced**
2 **tablespoons lemon juice**
½ **teaspoon *each* salt and dry basil**
½ **pint (1 cup) sour cream**
1 **cup (4 oz.) *each* shredded jack cheese and Cheddar cheese**
About 1½ **pounds broccoli**
1 **package (12 oz.) spinach noodles**
Boiling salted water
⅓ **cup chopped walnuts or sunflower seeds**

Melt butter in a wide frying pan over medium heat. Add onion and mushrooms and cook, stirring occasionally, until soft (about 8 minutes). Remove from heat and stir in lemon juice, salt, basil, sour cream, and ½ cup *each* of the jack cheese and Cheddar cheese. Mix until blended, then set aside.

Cut broccoli into small flowerets and thinly slice stems. Steam broccoli just until crisp-tender (about 5 minutes). Cook noodles in a large kettle of boiling salted water according to package directions; drain.

In a large bowl, combine sour cream mixture, noodles, and broccoli. Turn into a shallow 3-quart baking dish.

Bake casserole, covered, in a 350° oven for 30 minutes (40 minutes, if refrigerated). Remove from oven, sprinkle remaining cheese and walnuts over top, and continue baking, uncovered, for about 5 minutes or until cheese melts. Makes 8 servings.

Per serving: 20 grams protein, 46 grams carbohydrate, 64 milligrams cholesterol, 461 calories.

Savory Kugel

This baked noodle dish originated with a Russian-Jewish version of unsweetened noodle pudding.

Spinach noodles give it color and there's a touch of seasoning to spark the flavor.

8 **ounces packaged spinach noodles**
Boiling salted water
1½ **cups large curd cottage cheese**
1 **cup (½ pint) sour cream**
1 **clove garlic, minced or pressed**
3 **green onions (including tops), thinly sliced**
1 **teaspoon Worcestershire**
¼ **teaspoon liquid hot pepper seasoning**
2 **tablespoons butter or margarine, melted**
½ **cup grated Parmesan cheese**

Cook noodles in a large kettle of boiling salted water according to package directions. Drain, rinse with cold water, and drain again.

In a bowl, combine cottage cheese, sour cream, garlic, green onions, Worcestershire, hot pepper seasoning, and melted butter. Gently stir in noodles. Turn mixture into a greased 1½-quart casserole. Sprinkle Parmesan cheese over top. Bake, covered, in a 350° oven for about 30 minutes or until heated through. Makes 6 servings.

Per serving: 17 grams protein, 33 grams carbohydrate, 69 milligrams cholesterol, 334 calories.

Vegetable Kebabs

(Pictured on page 58)

If you are serving meat eaters as well as vegetarians at your next barbecue, plan on Vegetable Kebabs for everyone. It's hard for even a meat-and-potato buff to resist them. To accompany these skewers of herb-marinated vegetables, you might serve a Greek-style salad of crisp greens, tomatoes, olives, and feta cheese, along with pilaf and garlic bread.

(Continued on page 59)

Vegetable Kebabs (cont'd.)

1 **small unpeeled eggplant (about ¾ lb.), cut into 2-inch cubes**

2 **large carrots, cut into ½-inch slices**

About 1 dozen **small thin-skinned potatoes (2 inches in diameter)**

3 **medium-size zucchini, cut crosswise into 1-inch slices**

2 **small red or green bell peppers, seeded and cut into 1-inch squares**

1 **large onion, cut in wedges and layers separated**

About 16 **whole large mushrooms**

Herb Marinade (recipe follows)

Salt

Cook eggplant in 1 inch boiling water for 3 minutes; drain. Cook carrots in 1 inch boiling water until crisp-tender (about 6 minutes); drain. Cook unpeeled potatoes in 1 inch boiling water just until tender (about 20 minutes); drain and cut in half.

Place eggplant, carrots, potatoes, zucchini, bell peppers, onion, and mushrooms in a plastic bag. Prepare herb marinade; pour over vegetables. Seal bag and refrigerate for 2 hours or until next day.

Drain and reserve marinade from vegetables. Onto 8 sturdy metal skewers, alternately thread vegetables. Place on a lightly greased grill 4 to 6 inches above a solid bed of low-glowing coals. Cook, turning often and basting with reserved marinade, for 10 to 15 minutes or until vegetables are tender. Sprinkle lightly with salt before serving. (Remaining marinade

can be refrigerated up to 2 weeks and used again.) Makes 4 servings of 2 skewers each.

Per serving: 12 grams protein, 71 grams carbohydrate, no cholesterol, 385 calories.

Herb Marinade. In a bowl, combine ¾ cup **salad oil**; ¼ cup **white wine vinegar**; 2 cloves **garlic** (minced or pressed); 1 teaspoon *each* **Dijon mustard, dry basil,** and **oregano** leaves; ½ teaspoon *each* **marjoram** leaves and **dry rosemary**; and ¼ teaspoon **pepper**.

Stuffed Chard or Grape Leaves

These toothsome little rolls take on a different character depending on their wrapper. Chard wrappers have a pleasant bitter flavor that contrasts with the filling of fruit, nuts, and rice. Grape leaves lend a more pickled, winy flavor.

¼ **cup olive oil or salad oil**

¼ **cup pine nuts or slivered almonds**

2 **large onions, chopped**

½ **cup chopped parsley**

2 **cups cooked brown rice**

½ **cup raisins**

4 **teaspoons dill weed**

½ **teaspoon *each* salt and ground cinnamon**

¾ **teaspoon ground allspice**

⅛ **teaspoon ground red pepper (cayenne)**

1 **tablespoon lemon juice**

40 **small or 20 large Swiss chard leaves, or 1 jar (8 oz.) grape leaves**

2 **tablespoons water**

Heat oil in a wide frying pan over medium heat; add nuts and cook, stirring, until golden. Remove nuts with a slotted spoon and set aside. Add onions to pan and cook, stirring frequently, until golden brown (15 to 20 minutes). Add parsley and cook for 2 minutes. Remove

pan from heat and stir in rice, raisins, dill, salt, cinnamon, allspice, red pepper, and lemon juice. Stir gently to blend.

If using chard, wash leaves, cut off stems, and save for another use. Cut large leaves in half lengthwise; leave small leaves whole. Drop leaves into a large kettle of boiling water and blanch for 1 minute; drain. Plunge leaves into a bowl of cold water to cool, then drain again. Spread leaves, veined side down, on a flat surface. Place 1 scant tablespoon filling near stem end, fold in leaf's sides, and roll up.

If using grape leaves, drain, rinse with cold water, and drain again. Spread leaves, veined side up, on a flat surface; cut off stems. Place 1 scant tablespoon filling near stem end, fold sides in, then roll up.

Arrange filled leaves, seam side down, in a single layer in a greased baking pan. Sprinkle with the water. If made ahead, cover and refrigerate. Bake, covered, in a 350° oven for about 25 minutes (35 minutes, if refrigerated) or until hot. Makes 8 servings.

Per serving: 5 grams protein, 29 grams carbohydrate, no cholesterol, 206 calories.

Sesame Tofu Sticks

Marinated in teriyaki sauce and coated in a sesame seed mixture, these tofu sticks come out crusty on the outside but remain creamy on the inside. Steamed or stir-fried vegetables and rice or pilaf would go well with this dish.

About 1 pound **medium-firm tofu**

Teriyaki Sauce (recipe follows)

½ **cup whole wheat flour**

¼ **cup sesame seeds**

2 **tablespoons salad oil**

3 **green onions (including tops), thinly sliced**

(Continued on next page)

Everything tastes better when it's grilled outdoors—including herb-marinated Vegetable Kebabs (recipe on page 57 and above). Add Fruited Rice Pilaf (recipe on page 67), and Hummus (recipe on page 14) to scoop up with whole wheat pocket bread, and you have a perfect Middle Eastern vegetarian barbecue.

. . . Sesame Tofu Sticks (cont'd.)

Place tofu in a colander and let drain for 10 minutes. Meanwhile, prepare teriyaki sauce. Cut tofu in domino-shaped pieces and marinate in teriyaki sauce for 15 minutes, turning to coat well. Meanwhile, combine flour and sesame seeds. Lift tofu from marinade, drain briefly, then dip in flour mixture to coat all sides.

Heat 1 tablespoon of the oil in a wide frying pan over medium heat; add half the tofu and cook until lightly browned (about 4 minutes on each side). Remove from pan and keep warm. Add the remaining 1 tablespoon oil to cook the remaining tofu. Serve warm, sprinkled with green onion, and pass remaining teriyaki sauce for dipping. Makes 4 servings.

Per serving: 14 grams protein, 12 grams carbohydrate, no cholesterol, 293 calories.

Teriyaki Sauce. Combine ⅓ cup **soy sauce**, 2 tablespoons *each* **sugar** and **dry sherry**, ¾ teaspoon grated **fresh ginger** or ¼ teaspoon ground ginger, and 2 cloves **garlic** (minced or pressed).

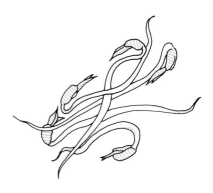

Mushroom Cabbage Rolls

We found the long, broad leaves of Chinese cabbage easier to roll than regular cabbage. If you can't buy Chinese cabbage, core a whole head of regular cabbage and steam it for 5 minutes. When it's cool, carefully peel off the large outer leaves to use in this recipe.

1 large head (about 3 lbs.) Chinese cabbage (napa cabbage)
1 tablespoon *each* salad oil and butter or margarine
1 pound mushrooms, sliced
1 large onion, chopped
1 clove garlic, minced or pressed
1½ cups cooked wheat berries (page 73) or cooked brown rice
½ teaspoon salt
Dash of pepper
1 cup (4 oz.) shredded jack cheese
⅓ cup grated Parmesan cheese
Fresh Tomato Sauce (page 54) or 1 jar (about 15 oz.) meatless marinara sauce

Cut off core end of cabbage and remove torn outer leaves. Separate remaining leaves and select 12 large ones (save inside leaves for another use). In a large kettle of boiling salted water, cook 3 or 4 of these large leaves at a time just until limp (about 2 minutes). Lift from water and let drain and cool.

Heat salad oil and butter in a wide frying pan over medium-high heat. Add mushrooms, onion, and garlic; cook, stirring occasionally, until vegetables are soft and pan juices have evaporated. Stir in wheat berries, salt, and pepper; cook for 1 minute. Remove pan from heat and stir in jack cheese and Parmesan.

Spoon an equal amount of filling onto base of each leaf, and roll halfway to enclose. Fold sides in, then continue rolling up. Place rolls, seam side down, in a shallow 2-quart baking dish. If made ahead, cover and refrigerate.

Bake, covered, in a 350° oven for 30 minutes (40 minutes, if refrigerated) or until hot throughout. Heat tomato sauce or marinara sauce to spoon over each serving. Makes six servings of 2 rolls each.

Per serving (including fresh tomato sauce): 15 grams protein, 27 grams carbohydrate, 30 milligrams cholesterol, 259 calories.

Armenian Vegetable Casserole ✓

French cooks have their ratatouille; Armenian cooks have this hearty vegetable dish, called *tourlu*. You can serve it in wide soup bowls with a mound of yogurt on top to melt down into the marvelous juices.

½ pound green beans
1 medium-size (about 1 lb.) eggplant, unpeeled, and cut into 1-inch cubes
2 large onions, cut into 1-inch cubes
3 medium-size carrots, cut into ¾-inch-thick slanting slices
2 large stalks celery, cut into ½-inch thick slices
1 large red or green bell pepper, seeded, cut into 1-inch squares
2 large thin-skinned potatoes, peeled and cut into 1½-inch cubes
1 can (about 1 lb.) pear-shaped tomatoes
¼ cup olive oil or salad oil
½ cup catsup
About 2 teaspoons salt
1½ teaspoons *each* sugar and dry basil
¼ teaspoon pepper
3 small zucchini
1 cup plain yogurt

Snap off ends of beans and cut into 2-inch lengths. Combine in a 5-quart or larger casserole with eggplant, onions, carrots, celery, bell pepper, and potatoes.

Drain juice from tomatoes into casserole. Chop tomatoes and add to casserole, along with olive oil, catsup, salt, sugar, basil, and pepper; stir gently. Cover casserole and bake in a 350° oven for 1½ hours or until vegetables are almost tender, removing lid and basting vegetables with juices about every 30 minutes.

Meanwhile, remove ends of zucchini; cut zucchini into ½-inch slices. Remove casserole from oven and gently mix in zucchini. Return to oven and bake, uncovered, for 20 to 30 minutes or until vegetables are tender. Serve hot or at room temperature with a generous spoonful of yogurt on each serving. Makes 8 servings.

Per serving: 6 grams protein, 29 grams carbohydrate, 2 milligrams cholesterol, 198 calories.

Savory Vegetables & Tofu

(Pictured on page 74)

Try cooking your vegetables the Chinese way—in seasoned liquid. It lets vegetables keep their color while they absorb flavor from the liquid. To serve, arrange the vegetables in a ring and place a tofu-mushroom mélange in the center.

About 1 pound medium-firm tofu

Cooking Sauce (recipe follows)

½ **teaspoon salt**

1 **pound broccoli, green beans, or carrots**

4 **cups water**

1 **teaspoon *each* salt and sugar**

2 **quarter-size slices fresh ginger, crushed**

1 **tablespoon *each* salad oil and dry sherry**

4 **tablespoons salad oil**

¼ **pound mushrooms, quartered**

1 **tablespoon dry sherry**

½ **teaspoon sugar**

Place tofu in a colander and let drain for 15 minutes. Meanwhile, prepare cooking sauce and set aside. Cut tofu in domino-shaped pieces, and place between paper towels; gently press out excess water. Sprinkle with the ½ teaspoon salt and set aside.

If you use broccoli, cut off flowerets (if large, cut in half) and slash stems. Peel thick stalks and thinly slice. If you use green beans,

remove ends and strings; cut in 2-inch-long slanting slices. If you use carrots, cut in ¼-inch-thick slanting slices.

In a 3-quart pan over medium heat, place water, the 1 teaspoon *each* salt and sugar, ginger, and the 1 tablespoon *each* oil and sherry. Bring to a simmer.

Heat 2 tablespoons of the salad oil in a wide frying pan over high heat. Add mushrooms and cook, stirring, until golden. Add sherry and the ½ teaspoon sugar and cook until liquid evaporates; remove mushrooms and set aside. Reduce heat to medium and add the remaining 2 tablespoons oil. Add tofu and cook until flecked with brown (about 3 minutes on each side). Return mushrooms to pan. Stir cooking sauce, pour into pan, and cook, stirring gently, until sauce bubbles and thickens. Keep hot.

Bring seasoned water to a boil. Drop in vegetables. Cook until crisp-tender (about 4 minutes); drain, then discard ginger. To serve, arrange vegetables around edges of a serving platter. Pour tofu mixture into center. Makes 4 servings.

Per serving: 14 grams protein, 15 grams carbohydrate, .4 milligrams cholesterol, 299 calories.

Cooking Sauce. In a bowl, blend ½ cup **vegetable stock** (page 25), 2 tablespoons **soy sauce**, 1 tablespoon **dry sherry**, 1 teaspoon **sugar**, 2 teaspoons **cornstarch**, and ¼ teaspoon **sesame oil**.

Creamy Spinach-Artichoke Casserole

Just to prove once again that vegetarian cooking doesn't have to be time-consuming, here's a quick but elegant casserole that can be assembled ahead and baked when your guests arrive.

1 **jar (6½ oz.) marinated artichoke hearts**

¼ **pound mushrooms, thinly sliced**

1 **small onion, chopped**

1 **clove garlic, minced or pressed**

2 **packages (10 oz. *each*) frozen chopped spinach, thawed**

1 **can (10½ oz.) condensed cream of mushroom soup**

½ **cup sour cream**

2 **eggs, beaten**

¼ **teaspoon *each* oregano leaves, ground nutmeg, and white pepper**

½ **teaspoon lemon juice**

1 **cup crushed seasoned croutons**

Drain artichoke hearts, reserving marinade; set artichokes aside. Place marinade in a wide frying pan and add mushrooms, onion, and garlic. Cook over medium-high heat, stirring occasionally, until onion is limp. Remove pan from heat.

Squeeze spinach to remove moisture. Add spinach to mushroom mixture along with soup, sour cream, eggs, oregano, nutmeg, pepper, and lemon juice. Stir until well blended.

Spoon half the spinach mixture into a greased 1½-quart shallow casserole. Arrange artichokes on top and spoon remaining spinach mixture over them. Sprinkle crushed croutons over the top. Bake, uncovered, in a 325° oven for 35 to 40 minutes or until custard is set. Let stand for 5 minutes before serving. Makes 6 servings.

Per serving: 7 grams protein, 17 grams carbohydrate, 96 milligrams cholesterol, 171 calories.

Almond-Rice Stuffed Peppers

Brown rice or wheat berries give the stuffing for these peppers a satisfying chewiness. You might serve them with steamed broccoli and Quick Corn Bread (page 78). Double Mushroom Soup (page 27) would be a good first course.

- **3 large red or green bell peppers**
  Boiling water
- **2 cups cooked brown rice or wheat berries (page 73)**
- **¾ cup chopped almonds**
- **2 green onions (including tops) thinly sliced**
- **1 large tomato, peeled, seeded, and chopped**
- **¼ cup chopped parsley**
- **1½ cups (6 oz.) shredded Cheddar cheese**
- **2 eggs, lightly beaten**
- **½ teaspoon *each* Worcestershire and dry basil**
  Garlic salt
  Pepper

Cut peppers lengthwise through stems; remove stems and seeds. Drop pepper halves into boiling water; boil, uncovered, for 2 minutes, then plunge into cold water and drain well.

Stir together rice, almonds, green onions, tomato, parsley, 1 cup of the cheese, eggs, Worcestershire, basil, and garlic salt and pepper to taste. Mound mixture into pepper shells. Place peppers in a shallow baking pan; sprinkle tops equally with remaining ½ cup cheese. If made ahead, cover and refrigerate.

Bake, uncovered, in a 375° oven for about 35 minutes (45 minutes, if refrigerated) or until filling is piping hot. Makes 6 servings.

Per serving: 15 grams protein, 22 grams carbohydrate, 112 milligrams cholesterol, 320 calories.

India-spiced Eggplant

(Pictured on facing page)

In India, most curried foods are seasoned with individual spices rather than curry powder, and this eggplant dish is no exception. The various spices meld into a flavor that's distinctive, delicious, and not overly hot. This is especially good topped with raita—a yogurt-based salad (page 47).

- **1 large eggplant or 2 small ones (2 pounds *total*)**
- **2 tablespoons salad oil**
- **½ teaspoon cumin seeds**
- **1 tablespoon minced fresh ginger**
- **1 medium-size red onion, coarsely sliced**
- **1 teaspoon turmeric**
- **½ green pepper, seeded and coarsely chopped**
- **2 teaspoons ground coriander**
- **1 teaspoon *each* ground cumin, paprika, and salt**
- **¼ teaspoon black pepper**
- **1 large tomato, peeled and chopped**
- **¼ cup water**
- **¼ cup coarsely chopped fresh coriander (cilantro)**

Place whole eggplant in a shallow pan and bake in a 400° oven until very soft (about 50 minutes). Cool slightly. Cut a slit in eggplant and scoop out pulp; discard large seed pockets, skin, and stem. Coarsely chop pulp; place in a colander to drain.

Heat oil in a wide frying pan over medium heat. Add cumin seeds, ginger, and onion and cook, stirring occasionally, until onion is soft. Stir in turmeric, green pepper, coriander, ground cumin, paprika, salt, pepper, and tomato. Cook, stirring occasionally, until tomato releases its juices (about 5 minutes). Add water and bring to a simmer. Reduce heat to low and simmer, uncovered, for 10 minutes. Stir in chopped eggplant and cook for 5 minutes to heat through and blend flavors. Just before serving, stir in coriander. Makes 6 servings.

Per serving: 2 grams protein, 11 grams carbohydrate, no cholesterol, 80 calories.

Vegetable Curry

(Pictured on facing page)

This Indian curry takes easily to improvisation. You start with a basic method of cooking and combination of spices, then add vegetables that appeal to you. If you cook vegetables other than those suggested here, and the textures vary, add the firmest vegetables to the pan first. Then, toward the end of the cooking time, add the more tender vegetables.

- **2 tablespoons salad oil**
- **1 large onion, coarsely chopped**
- **1 teaspoon *each* salt and curry powder**
- **½ teaspoon pepper**
- **¼ teaspoon *each* ground ginger and cumin**
- **⅛ teaspoon ground red pepper (cayenne)**
- **2 bay leaves**
- **2 medium-size carrots, cut into ¼-inch slices**
- **½ pound green beans, cut into 2-inch lengths**
- **1 red or green bell pepper, seeded and cut into 1-inch pieces**
- **½ small cauliflower, separated into flowerets**
- **½ pound broccoli, separated into flowerets, stems peeled and sliced**
- **½ pound butternut or banana squash, peeled and cut into 1-inch pieces**
- **¾ cup water**

Pour oil into a 5-quart pan and place over medium heat. Add

(Continued on page 64)

__Feast from India__ features, clockwise from top left, deep-fried bread called Puris (page 81), Vegetable Curry (above), India-spiced Eggplant (at left) encircled by fried mint leaves, and Savory Fried Rice (page 64). Small bowls contain Raita— Mint & Coriander, and Cucumber & Tomato; recipes are on page 47.

onion and cook, stirring occasionally, until soft. Stir in salt, curry powder, pepper, ginger, cumin, and red pepper; cook for 1 minute. Add bay leaves, carrots, beans, bell pepper, cauliflower, broccoli, squash, and water. Cover and bring to a boil; reduce heat and simmer until vegetables are just tender (about 20 minutes). Remove cover, increase heat, and cook for a few minutes to reduce pan juices by one-half. Remove bay leaves before serving. Makes 6 servings.

Per serving: 5 grams protein, 33 grams carbohydrate, no cholesterol, 127 calories.

Savory Fried Rice

(Pictured on page 63)

This spicy rice and vegetable dish from India is a dazzling yellow, thanks to turmeric. Savory Fried Rice can be an entrée on its own, or it can share the honors with steamed vegetables or a curried dish.

1½ cups long-grain rice
6 whole cloves
3 whole black peppers
¼ teaspoon turmeric
½ teaspoon salt
2½ cups water
6 whole cardamom seeds
2 small leeks
2 tablespoons butter or margarine
1 medium-size carrot, shredded
1 cup frozen peas, thawed
¼ cup *each* cashews and raisins
3 hard-cooked eggs, cut in wedges (optional)

Place rice, cloves, black peppers, turmeric, salt, and water in a 2-quart pan. Crush cardamom seeds slightly with your fingers and add both husks and seeds to rice.

Cover pan and bring to a boil over high heat. Reduce heat to low and simmer, covered, until rice is tender and liquid is absorbed (about 20 minutes).

Meanwhile, wash and trim leeks. Cut crosswise in ½-inch-thick slices; use the tender part of the green tops as well as the white. Separate the white part into rings. Melt butter in a wide frying pan over medium heat. Add leeks and carrot and cook, stirring occasionally, for 5 minutes. Add peas, cashews, and raisins and cook for 3 minutes.

When rice is cooked, stir in leek mixture. Turn onto a serving platter and garnish with egg wedges if desired. Makes 6 servings.

Per serving (including eggs): 9 grams protein, 49 grams carbohydrate, 138 milligrams cholesterol, 321 calories.

Baked Lentils with Cheese

Lentils and vegetables bake together in this well-seasoned casserole. During the last few minutes, you stir in cheese to complement the taste—and the protein.

1 package (12 oz.) lentils, rinsed
2 cups water
1 bay leaf
2 teaspoons salt
¼ teaspoon *each* pepper, and marjoram, sage, and thyme leaves
2 large onions, chopped
2 cloves garlic, minced or pressed
1 can (about 1 lb.) tomatoes
2 large carrots, cut in ⅛-inch-thick slices
1 stalk celery, thinly sliced
1 green pepper, seeded and chopped
2 tablespoons chopped parsley
1½ cups (6 oz.) shredded sharp Cheddar cheese

Place lentils in a shallow 3-quart casserole or 9 by 13-inch baking dish along with water, bay leaf, salt, pepper, marjoram, sage, thyme, onions, garlic, and tomatoes (break up with a spoon) and their liquid.

Bake, covered, in a 375° oven for 30 minutes. Remove from oven and stir in carrots and celery. Cover and bake for about 40 more minutes or until vegetables are tender. Remove from oven and stir in green pepper and parsley; sprinkle cheese on top. Return to oven and bake, uncovered, for 5 more minutes or until cheese is melted. Makes 6 servings.

Per serving: 26 grams protein, 55 grams carbohydrate, 28 milligrams cholesterol, 402 calories.

Ricotta-stuffed Squash

(Pictured on page 66)

The favorite flavors of Italian cooking season this ricotta-spinach filling for zucchini, crookneck, or pattypan squash. A whole-grain pilaf or buttered pasta sprinkled with Parmesan cheese would be excellent with this dish.

8 crookneck or zucchini squash (*each* about 6 inches long), or 8 large pattypan squash
2 tablespoons butter or margarine
1 small onion, finely chopped
1 clove garlic, minced or pressed
1 package (10 oz.) frozen chopped spinach, thawed
2 eggs
2 cups (1 lb.) ricotta cheese
¼ cup grated Parmesan cheese
1 tablespoon chopped parsley
½ teaspoon *each* salt, dry basil, and oregano leaves
Dash of pepper
Tomato Sauce (recipe follows)

Trim ends off squash; cut squash in half lengthwise. With a teaspoon scoop out seeds and part of pulp (save pulp for soup stock), leaving shells ½ inch thick. Steam squash shells over boiling water until crisp-tender (about 5 minutes). Plunge in cold water, drain well, and set aside.

In a small frying pan over medium heat, melt 1 tablespoon of the butter. Add onion and garlic and cook, stirring occasionally, until onion is limp. Squeeze spinach to remove excess moisture. Add spinach to onion mixture and cook for 1 minute; let cool.

In a bowl, combine eggs with ricotta, stirring until well blended. Stir in Parmesan, parsley, salt, basil, oregano, pepper, and spinach mixture. Allowing about 3 tablespoons filling per squash, mound filling inside squash shells. Arrange filled shells in shallow baking pans. Melt the remaining 1 tablespoon butter; brush over cut surfaces of squash. If made ahead, cover and refrigerate.

Bake, uncovered, in a 350° oven for about 20 minutes (30 minutes, if refrigerated) or until filling is piping hot. While squash is baking, prepare tomato sauce to spoon over squash before serving. Makes 8 servings.

Per serving (including tomato sauce): 13 grams protein, 10 grams carbohydrate, 95 milligrams cholesterol, 184 calories.

Tomato Sauce. In a 1-quart pan, simmer together for 5 minutes 1 can (15 oz.) **tomato sauce,** 2 tablespoons chopped **parsley,** 1 clove **garlic** (minced), 1 teaspoon **dry basil,** ½ teaspoon **oregano leaves,** and **salt** and **pepper** to taste.

 # Recipe Adaptations for Meat Eaters

Many of the recipes in this book can be adapted for meat eaters. We point this out because many people looking into vegetarian cooking for health or budget reasons want to reduce the amount of meat in their diets, but don't want to eliminate it completely. Some continue to eat small quantities of all types of meat; others confine themselves to chicken and fish.

Sometimes only one or two members of a household want to eat meatless meals. Teenagers interested in vegetarian diets are often confronted with the practical objection that it's too much trouble to cook two separate kinds of food. This leaves them to fend for themselves or glower through family meals and make disparaging remarks about carnivores.

Here are some suggestions for adapting the recipes in this book to satisfy families with a member who eats to the beat of a different drum. The adaptations will also please those cutting back, but not eliminating meat from their diet. An added bonus is that most of the adaptations are budget stretchers making good use of leftover meat. Remember that the addition of meat will invalidate the nutritional data which follows each recipe, increasing protein, cholesterol, and calories.

Soups. For the vegetarian in the family, reserve a portion of soup before adding meat. We suggest adding 1 cup shredded cooked pork to Hot & Sour Soup (page 29); 1 can (8 oz.) minced clams, drained, to Tomato Corn Chowder (page 29); 1 cup diced cooked ham to Lemony Lentil Soup (page 30); sliced and browned Italian sausage to Fresh Vegetable Basil Soup (page 33).

Salads. Add 1 cup diced cooked chicken to all or part of Zucchini Fiesta Salad (page 19). Fill half the Salad-in-a-Boat (page 19) with your favorite chicken or ham salad, half with egg salad. Serve the Bulgur Supper Salad (page 20) surrounded by pieces of roast chicken or slices of roast beef or lamb. Add 1 cup small cooked shrimp to Quick Artichoke Pasta Salad (page 21). Garnish half of Perfect Protein Salad (page 16) with slivers of roast beef.

Entrées. Most vegetarian entrées can be served in smaller portions to accompany roast beef, chicken, lamb, or fish. You can add diced cooked chicken or beef to Almond-Rice Stuffed Peppers (page 61). Add cooked ground beef to Bulgur Mexicana (page 52), Mushroom Cabbage Rolls (page 60), or Cracked Wheat Vegetable Pilaf (page 67). Green Enchiladas (page 51) can be filled with cooked chicken or ground beef; Sonora Pizza (page 52) can have a layer of cooked ground beef added to the toppings.

Stir-fry strips of beef to accompany Savory Vegetables & Tofu (page 61), or marinate chicken wings in the same teriyaki sauce you use for Sesame Tofu Sticks (page 59), then bake.

Cooked ground lamb can be rolled up in some of the Stuffed Chard or Grape Leaves (page 59). You can make Whole Wheat Zucchini Pizza (page 54) as a combination order: half vegetarian, half pepperoni or sausage. Layered Chili (page 49) can be made *con carne* with ground beef.

Cracked Wheat Vegetable Pilaf

Soaking instead of cooking is a traditional Middle Eastern way to prepare bulgur—that way the grains stay separate and slightly chewy, even when baked in this colorful pilaf.

- **1 cup bulgur wheat**
- **1 cup boiling vegetable stock (page 25)**
- **2 tablespoons chopped parsley**
- **¼ cup diced green or red bell pepper or carrot**
- **3 green onions (including tops), thinly sliced**
- **2 cups (8 oz.) shredded Cheddar or jack cheese**
- **1 cup whole kernel corn, cut off cob, or frozen and thawed**
- **1 egg, lightly beaten**
- **1 can (8 oz.) tomato sauce**
- **1 teasoon dry basil**
- **½ teaspoon *each* oregano leaves and garlic salt**
- **¼ teaspoon pepper**

In a large bowl, combine bulgur and stock. Stirring occasionally, let stand for about 1 hour or until liquid is absorbed. Stir in parsley, bell pepper, onions, cheese, corn, and egg. Add tomato sauce, basil, oregano, garlic salt, and pepper and stir gently. Spoon into a shallow greased 1½-quart casserole. Cover and bake in a 350° oven until heated through (25 to 30 minutes). Makes 6 servings.

Per serving: 15 grams protein, 14 grams carbohydrate, 80 milligrams cholesterol, 312 calories.

Like a sunburst of flavor, arrangement of Ricotta-stuffed Squash (recipe on page 64) around Brown Rice & Carrot Pilaf (recipe on this page) radiates the warmth of good cooking. Pass tomato sauce to spoon over the squash.

Stuffed Zucchini

Stuff extra large zucchini with Cracked Wheat Vegetable Pilaf for an impressive main dish.

Cracked Wheat Vegetable Pilaf (preceding recipe)
3 large zucchini, *each* about 10 inches long and 2 inches wide

Prepare pilaf to the point of baking.

Trim ends of zucchini; cut each zucchini in half lengthwise. Using a spoon, scoop out seeds. Mound pilaf into zucchini halves; place in two 9 by 13-inch pans. Pour about ¼ inch water into each pan.

Bake zucchini, uncovered, in a 375° oven for 35 to 40 minutes or until tender and pilaf is hot. Makes 6 servings.

Per serving: 17 grams protein, 22 grams carbohydrate, 80 milligrams cholesterol, 351 calories.

Fruited Rice Pilaf

(Pictured on page 58)

Brown rice, raisins, dried apricots, dates, and cashews—what a wonderful mixture. You can serve it with Vegetable Kebabs or simply surround it with golden chunks of steamed butternut squash. A yogurt side dish of raita (page 47) would be perfect.

- **1 cup long-grain brown rice**
- **½ teaspoon salt**
- **2 cups vegetable stock (page 25)**
- **2 tablespoons butter or margarine**
- **¼ cup cashews**
- **¼ cup *each* raisins and coarsely chopped dried apricots and pitted dates**

In a 2-quart pan, combine rice, salt, and vegetable stock. Cover and bring to a boil over high heat. Reduce heat to low; and simmer until rice is tender and liquid is absorbed (about 45 minutes).

Meanwhile, in a small frying pan over medium-low heat, melt butter. Add nuts and cook until golden. Remove from pan with a slotted spoon and set aside. Add raisins, apricots, and dates to pan and cook, stirring, for 2 minutes.

When rice is cooked, stir in dried fruits; cover and let stand for 5 minutes. Stir in nuts just before serving. Makes 6 servings.

Per serving: 4 grams protein, 39 grams carbohydrate, 12 milligrams cholesterol, 230 calories.

Brown Rice & Carrot Pilaf

(Pictured on facing page)

Onion and carrot give a pleasant sweetness to this easy pilaf. If you wish to add a crunchy texture, stir in sprouts just before serving.

- **3 tablespoons butter or margarine**
- **1 large onion, finely chopped**
- **1 cup coarsely shredded carrots**
- **1 cup long-grain brown rice**
- **2½ cups vegetable stock (page 25)**
- **½ teaspoon salt**
- **½ cup chopped parsley**
- **2 cups bean sprouts (optional)**

Melt butter in a 2-quart pan over medium-high heat. Add onion and carrots and cook until onion is soft (about 5 minutes). Stir in rice; continue to cook, stirring, until rice begins to brown slightly. Add stock and salt; cover and simmer until rice is tender and liquid is absorbed (about 45 minutes). Stir in parsley and sprouts, if used, just before serving. Makes 6 servings.

Per serving (including sprouts): 4 grams protein, 32 grams carbohydrates, 31 milligrams cholesterol, 198 calories.

Vegetable Side Dishes

Because ideas for preparing and serving vegetables are always welcome, we've gathered in this section some recipes for quick sauces to dress plain vegetables, and for vegetable combination dishes to give variety to your menus. First, though, we explain in detail two important cooking methods—stir-frying and steaming—that can be adapted to almost any fresh vegetable.

How to Stir-fry

As a technique for cooking vegetables, stir-frying is one of the best. A wok is the traditional piece of equipment to use, but a wide frying pan works, too. You begin by cutting your vegetables into uniform shapes—usually thin slices or pieces that will cook in a few minutes.

To stir-fry, place a wok or wide frying pan over high heat. When the pan is hot, add 1 to 2 tablespoons salad oil for each 1 pound of cut vegetables, and swirl the oil around the pan. When the oil is hot, you can add seasonings, if you wish—such as 1 clove minced garlic and ½ teaspoon minced fresh ginger—and cook just until fragrant. Then add the cut vegetables

and stir-fry for 1 minute to coat them with oil. If you don't wish to add seasonings, add the vegetables to the pan as soon as the oil is hot.

What you do next depends on the vegetable. With a few, such as bean sprouts or tomato or onion wedges, you continue cooking for about another minute. Most vegetables, though, need a little liquid to become tender. Pour in 1 to 3 tablespoons water; then cover and continue cooking until vegetables are crisp-tender. Plan on 2 to 3 minutes for asparagus, bok choy, green peppers, snow peas, and zucchini. More dense vegetables, such as broccoli, carrots, cauliflower, and green beans, should be cooked for 3 to 5 minutes.

If the pan appears dry, add a few more drops water; cover and continue cooking until crisp-tender. You want the vegetables to steam lightly, not to simmer in liquid. The cooking times and amounts of water should be used as flexible guidelines, because the way you cut a vegetable and the intensity of the heat you use both affect the cooking time.

If you wish to cook several vegetables and the textures are different, add firmer vegetables to the pan first and partially cook; then add the more tender vegetables near the end of the cooking time. Better yet, you can cook each vegetable separately and combine them for reheating and blending of flavors.

When the vegetable is cooked, season to taste with salt, pepper, and your favorite herbs; then serve piping hot. Or if you like to serve vegetables in the Chinese manner with a light sauce, combine ½ cup vegetable stock (page 25), 1 tablespoon cornstarch, and 2 teaspoons soy sauce. Add this to the pan of hot cooked vegetables and cook, stirring, until the sauce bubbles and thickens (about 30 seconds).

Cooking with Steam

While stir-frying is very active cooking, the opposite is true of steaming. You simply place vegetables *over* boiling water, then cover and let them steam for about the same length of time you would cook vegetables *in* the boiling water. Because swirling vapors, rather than water, tenderize the vegetables, there's little loss of vitamins and minerals.

Many types of steaming equipment are available, from compartmentalized steamers that let you steam several vegetables at a time, to bamboo steaming baskets that you set in a wok. One of the least expensive steamers is a collapsible metal steaming basket that you place inside another cooking pot.

Steamed vegetables have a light flavor. They need little seasoning to emphasize their freshness. If you wish, you can sprinkle them with salt, pepper, and herbs before cooking, or season them after cooking; finally, top them with butter or dress them with a flavorful sauce.

If you plan to serve steamed vegetables in a cold salad, or if you intend to marinate them for a first course, cool them quickly in cold water after cooking, then drain and refrigerate them.

Vegetable Sauces

To give a finished look and extra flavor to hot steamed vegetables, dress them with one of the following hot or cold sauces. For scale watchers, we've included some low-calorie variations of traditional sauces, too.

Herbed Tofu Sauce. Drain ½ carton (1-lb. 6-oz. size) **medium-firm tofu.** Pat tofu dry, place in a blender or food processor, and purée until completely smooth (about 5 minutes). Stir in 1¼ teaspoons **celery salt,** 1 tablespoon chopped **parsley,** ½ cup sliced **green onions,** 2 teaspoons **Dijon mustard,** 1 teaspoon prepared **horseradish,** ½ teaspoon **dill weed,** ¼ teaspoon **onion powder,** and 2 cloves **garlic,** pressed. Cover and refrigerate for at least 1 day to blend flavors. Serve cold. Makes 1¼ cups sauce.

Per tablespoon: 3 grams protein, 1 gram carbohydrate, no cholesterol, 28 calories.

Savory Cheese Sauce. In a blender or food processor, place 1 cup **cottage cheese,** ½ cup **plain yogurt,** 1 tablespoon **lemon juice,** 1 teaspoon **sugar,** ¼ teaspoon *each* **salt** and **dill weed,** a dash of **pepper,** and 2 tablespoons *each* chopped **onion** and chopped **parsley.** Purée until mixture is smooth. Serve cold. Makes 1½ cups.

Per tablespoon: 1.5 grams protein, 1 gram carbohydrate, 2 milligrams cholesterol, 13 calories.

Green Herb Sauce *(pictured on page 71).* In a blender, place ½ cup packed **watercress** leaves and small stems (or spinach leaves), ½ cup packed **parsley** sprigs, 1 large **shallot** or 1 large green onion and top (sliced), ½ teaspoon *each* **tarragon** and **thyme** leaves, ½ teaspoon **salt,** ¾ teaspoon **dry mustard,** 2 tablespoons **white wine vinegar,** and 1 **egg;** whirl until liquefied. With motor running,

begin pouring 1 cup **salad oil** into blender in a small stream; add oil very slowly at first, then a little faster as sauce begins to thicken. Serve cold. Makes 1⅔ cups.

Per tablespoon: .5 grams protein, .5 grams carbohydrate, 9 milligrams cholesterol, 82 calories.

Parmesan Sour Cottage Sauce *(pictured on page 71).* Place 1 pint (2 cups) **cottage cheese** in a fine wire strainer. Hold under cold running water and stir gently until water runs clear; let drain for about 20 minutes. Place cheese in a blender or food processor and add ¼ cup **skim milk** and 2 tablespoons **lemon juice.** Purée until completely smooth (about 5 minutes). Stir in ¼ cup grated **Parmesan** cheese and 2 tablespoons minced **green onion.** Serve cold. Makes 1½ cups.

Per tablespoon: 3 grams protein, 1 gram carbohydrate, 5 milligrams cholesterol, 25 calories.

Broiled Cheese Topping. In a bowl, combine ½ cup **mayonnaise,** ¼ cup grated **Parmesan cheese,** 2 tablespoons chopped **parsley,** and 2 teaspoons **lemon juice.** Beat 2 **egg whites** just until stiff, moist peaks form; fold into mayonnaise mixture. Spread topping evenly over 2 pounds hot steamed **vegetables,** such as green beans, broccoli, or asparagus. Broil, 6 to 8 inches from heat, until topping is golden brown. Serve hot. Makes 6 servings.

Per serving (including topping and vegetable): 5 grams protein, 9 grams carbohydrate, 16 milligrams cholesterol, 188 calories.

Yogurt Hollandaise *(pictured on page 71).* In the top of a double boiler, stir together 1 cup plain **yogurt** and 2 **whole eggs.** Add ¾ teaspoon **salt,** 1 teaspoon **sugar,** and ¼ teaspoon **liquid hot pepper seasoning.** Place over barely simmering water and cook, stirring constantly, until thickened (8 to 10 minutes). Serve hot.

(Continued on next page)

...Yogurt Hollandaise (cont'd.)

If made ahead, reheat, stirring, in top of double boiler over hot (not boiling) water. Makes 1⅓ cups.

Per tablespoon: 1 gram protein, 1 gram carbohydrate, 25 milligrams cholesterol, 14 calories.

Vegetable Combinations

The following recipes combine two vegetables or a vegetable with fruit, and they're especially delicious with grain entrées.

Curried Carrots with Fruit. Cut 4 **carrots** in ¼-inch-thick slanting slices; you should have 3 cups carrots. Drain 1 can (11 oz.) **mandarin oranges,** reserving 3 tablespoons of the liquid.

In a wide frying pan over medium-high heat, melt 2 tablespoons **butter** or margarine. Add carrots and reserved orange liquid. Cook, covered, until carrots are tender and most of liquid has evaporated (about 6 minutes).

In a cup, stir together 1 teaspoon **curry powder,** ½ teaspoon **salt,** and 1 teaspoon **lemon juice** until blended. Stir into carrots along with 1 cup whole seedless **grapes.** Cover and cook just until heated through. Stir in orange segments and 1 **green onion** (thinly sliced). Makes 6 servings.

Per serving: 1 gram protein, 17 grams carbohydrate, 12 milligrams cholesterol, 105 calories.

Stewed Tomatoes with Cheese. Drain a large (28-oz.) can **tomatoes** into a 2-quart pan. Coarsely chop tomatoes and add to pan. Cook, uncovered, over medium-high heat until a third of the liquid has evaporated. Season to taste with **salt** and **pepper.** Have ready ½ cup *each* diced **jack cheese** and **whole wheat croutons** and 2 tablespoons diced **green pepper.**

Just before serving, reheat tomatoes, add cheese, croutons, and green pepper, and stir just until cheese begins to melt. Makes 4 servings.

Per serving: 6 grams protein, 11 grams carbohydrate, 14 milligrams cholesterol, 106 calories.

Tomatoes Provençal. In a bowl, combine 1 tablespoon *each* finely chopped **garlic** (about 3 large cloves), chopped **parsley,** and fine dry **whole wheat bread crumbs,** ⅛ teaspoon **salt,** and a dash of **pepper.**

Core and halve 4 medium-size **tomatoes.** Squeeze gently to remove seeds and juice. Place tomatoes, cut side up, in a small baking dish. Drizzle with 1 tablespoon **olive oil** or salad oil. Bake, uncovered, in a 400° oven for 10 minutes. Sprinkle crumb mixture over tomatoes and continue baking for 15 minutes longer or until tomatoes are soft throughout. Makes 4 servings.

Per serving: 1.5 grams protein, 6 grams carbohydrate, .5 milligrams cholesterol, 57 calories.

Sun-gold Sprouts & Onions. Peel ½ pound small **white boiling onions;** score root end of each onion with a small cross. Wash and trim ½ pound **Brussels sprouts;** score stem end of each sprout with a small cross. Cut 1 small **carrot** crosswise into thin slices.

In a 3-quart pan over medium heat, bring 3 cups **water,** ½ teaspoon **salt,** and 1 teaspoon **sugar** to a boil. Add onions, reduce heat, and simmer, uncovered, for 15 minutes. Add sprouts and carrot and continue cooking, uncovered, for 8 minutes or until sprouts are crisp-tender. Drain. Add 1 tablespoon **butter** or margarine and a **dash** of pepper. Makes 4 servings.

Per serving: 3.5 grams protein, 11 grams carbohydrate, 9 milligrams cholesterol, 77 calories.

Winter Squash with Apples. Seed, peel, and cut 1 pound **winter squash** (acorn, butternut, banana, or Hubbard) into ½-inch cubes. You should have 4 cups. Peel and core 1 **apple** and cut into ½-inch cubes. Melt 3 tablespoons **butter** or margarine in a wide frying pan over medium-high heat. Add squash, apple, ¼ cup **water,** and 2 teaspoons **lemon juice.** Cover and cook, stirring occasionally, just until tender and liquid is absorbed (4 to 5 minutes). Stir in ¼ cup firmly packed **brown sugar,** ¼ teaspoon *each* **salt** and **ground cinnamon,** and ⅛ teaspoon **ground nutmeg.** Garnish with ¼ cup toasted sliced **almonds** just before serving. Makes 6 servings.

Per serving: 2 grams protein, 21 grams carbohydrate, 18 milligrams cholesterol, 154 calories.

Cauliflower with Broccoli Sauce. Remove flowerets from 1 pound **broccoli;** peel stems and slice. Steam stems and flowerets over boiling water until tender (10 to 12 minutes). Place broccoli in a blender and add ¼ cup **vegetable stock** (page 25), ½ cup **sour cream,** 1 tablespoon **lemon juice,** and ⅓ cup grated **Parmesan cheese.** Whirl until smooth. Season to taste with **salt** and **white pepper.**

Separate 1 medium-size head **cauliflower** into flowerets. Steam over boiling water until crisp-tender (10 to 12 minutes). Reheat broccoli sauce over low heat, then spoon sauce over cauliflower. Sprinkle ¼ cup **sunflower seeds** over the top. Makes 6 servings.

Per serving: 9 grams protein, 13 grams carbohydrate, 13 milligrams cholesterol, 122 calories.

A simple hot steamed vegetable— the freshest the season has to offer— goes to dinner in style with a special sauce. Clockwise from top right, you see Parmesan Sour Cottage Sauce, Yogurt Hollandaise, and Green Herb Sauce. The recipes are on page 69.

Breads & Breakfast

Moments to cherish: Buttering a still-warm slice of Wheat Berry Batter Bread (page 73) that's been filling your kitchen with an enticing aroma as it bakes. Passing around a platter of high-rising Cheddar Cheese Popovers (page 80). Tucking into a stack of Oatmeal Pancakes topped with Blueberry Sauce (page 84). Watching butter and syrup melt into the little indented squares on golden, light-textured Orange Yogurt Waffles (page 85).

This chapter is devoted to proving that it's pure pleasure to eat the nourishing-good whole grains so important in a vegetarian diet. The first section features breads, rolls, and muffins that can be part of almost any meal. Then the chapter focuses on breakfast foods, including granola-type cereals and some blender-quick breakfast beverages, as well as pancakes and waffles.

The collection of breads includes recipes for novices, plus recipes for more experienced bakers. Both beginners and old hands at bread baking will find the Whole Wheat Single-rising Dough (page 73) so versatile it might become their standard recipe for a variety of breads and rolls.

For sandwiches, you'll want to sample the attractive Pebble-top Oatmeal Bread (page 73), and the

lightly sweetened Maple-Molasses Bread (page 76).

If you want a bread with fruit in it, bake Anadama Bread (page 77), flavored with dates and banana; or try Apple Brown Bread (page 78), a quick bread that's delicious with cream cheese.

For breads with extra protein from cheese, there's a no-knead Casserole Cheese Bread (page 77) that bakes in individual loaves, and Honey-Wheat Buns (page 75) made with cottage cheese and bulgur wheat.

One of our special favorites is Chinese Steamed Buns (page 76). They're made with whole wheat flour and filled with a savory mixture of mushrooms and cashews. The buns are perfect with stir-fried vegetables.

Most of the recipes in this chapter call for whole wheat flour. You can use either the stone ground type (found in health food stores) or the standard whole wheat flour usually found in supermarkets. We find that stone ground whole wheat flour makes a denser loaf that takes a little longer to rise than the standard whole wheat flour. Freshness of the flour is also an important factor in successful bread baking: the fresher the flour—whether stone ground or standard—the better your final baked product will be.

Wheat Berry Batter Bread

If you're new to bread making and need the encouragement of fast results, this is the loaf for you. There's no kneading, and the golden-crusted result is a fine-textured bread studded with whole wheat kernels, called wheat berries.

Because wheat berries take time to precook, and can be used in so many ways, it makes sense to precook at least a cupful at a time. This will produce far more wheat berries than you'll need for one recipe, but you can use the extra cooked berries in pilaf or soup, or freeze them in small quantities for future loaves.

 1½ cups all-purpose flour
 1 tablespoon sugar
 ½ teaspoon salt
 1 package active dry yeast
 1 cup warm water (about 110°)
 ½ cup cooked, drained, wheat berries (directions follow)
 ¾ cup whole wheat flour
 Cornmeal
 1 tablespoon melted butter or margarine

In a bowl, combine all-purpose flour, sugar, salt, and yeast. Gradually beat in the warm water, then beat until dough is very elastic (about 3 minutes at medium speed if using electric mixer). Add wheat berries. Gradually beat in whole wheat flour (at low speed with electric mixer); dough should be very soft and elastic. Cover and let rise in a warm place until doubled (about 45 minutes).

Stir dough down with a wooden spoon. Grease a 4 by 8-inch loaf pan and coat with cornmeal; invert pan and shake out excess. Spoon dough into pan and spread in an even layer. Bake in a 375° oven for about 1 hour or until a skewer inserted in center of loaf comes out clean and crust is golden brown. Brush top with melted butter. Makes 1 loaf; cut into 16 slices.

Per slice: 2 grams protein, 15 grams carbohydrate, 2 milligrams cholesterol, 75 calories.

To precook wheat berries. In a large pan, combine 1 cup **wheat berries** and 5 cups **water**. Cover and let stand for at least 8 hours or until next day. (Or cover pan and bring to a boil over highest heat; boil for 2 minutes, then remove from heat and let stand, still covered, for 1 hour.)

Without draining wheat, bring to a boil over high heat. Reduce heat and simmer until tender (about 1½ hours). Drain well (save liquid for soup stock) and cool. Cover and store in refrigerator or freezer (thaw before using). Makes about 3 cups.

Pebble-top Oatmeal Bread

(Pictured as rolls on cover)

You can shape this even-textured bread into loaves or rolls to be crowned with an attractive pebble topping of rolled oats.

 1 package active dry yeast
 ¼ cup warm water (about 110°)
 ¼ cup molasses
 4 tablespoons butter or margarine
 2 teaspoons salt
 ¼ cup firmly packed brown sugar
 2½ cups regular or quick-cooking rolled oats
 1 cup *each* boiling water and cold water
 4½ to 5 cups all-purpose flour
 3 tablespoons milk

In a small bowl, combine yeast, the warm water, and 1 tablespoon of the molasses; let stand until bubbly (about 15 minutes). In a large bowl, combine butter, remaining molasses, salt, brown sugar, 2 cups of the oats, and boiling water; stir until butter melts. Add cold water

and yeast mixture. Beat in 4 cups of the flour, 1 cup at a time.

Turn dough out onto a floured board; knead until smooth and elastic (10 to 20 minutes), adding flour as needed to prevent sticking. Turn dough over in a greased bowl; cover and let rise in a warm place until doubled (about 1 hour). Punch dough down; knead briefly on a floured board to release air.

To make loaves, divide dough in half and shape each half into a loaf; place in greased 9 by 5-inch loaf pans.

To make rolls, divide dough into 20 equal pieces. Shape each piece into a smooth ball. Place balls about 2 inches apart on greased baking sheets and flatten slightly.

Soften remaining ½ cup rolled oats in milk; dot over tops of loaves or buns. Cover and let rise in a warm place until doubled (about 45 minutes).

Bake loaves in a 350° oven for about 1 hour or until bread sounds hollow when tapped. Turn out on a rack to cool. Bake buns in a 350° oven until lightly browned (15 to 18 minutes). Makes 2 loaves (cut 18 slices per loaf) or 20 buns.

Per slice: 3 grams protein, 19 grams carbohydrate, 8 milligrams cholesterol, 102 calories.

Per bun: 5 grams protein, 34 grams carbohydrate, 13 milligrams cholesterol, 183 calories.

Whole Wheat Single-rising Dough

(Pictured as crescent rolls on cover)

Even a dedicated bread baker appreciates a yeast dough as speedy as this one—it rises only once.

Its versatility is also a boon. You can bake all of the dough at once or refrigerate it for later baking. You can make the herb and cheese variation that follows the basic recipe. And you can make either dough into loaves or crescent rolls.

(Continued on page 75)

3 cups *each* all-purpose flour and whole wheat flour

½ cup wheat germ

2 packages active dry yeast

1 cup warm water (about 110°)

3 tablespoons sugar

3 teaspoons salt

1 cup warm milk (about 110°)

⅓ cup melted butter or margarine

2 eggs, lightly beaten

In a bowl, mix together all-purpose flour, whole wheat flour, and wheat germ. In a large bowl, dissolve yeast in the warm water. Add sugar, salt, milk, butter, and eggs. Beat in 3 cups of the flour mixture, 1 cup at a time, then beat until dough is elastic (about 5 minutes at medium speed if using electric mixer).

With a heavy-duty mixer or wooden spoon, gradually beat in remaining flour mixture. Dough should be soft, but not too sticky to knead; add additional all-purpose flour if necessary to prevent sticking. Turn dough out onto a floured board and knead just until smooth. Divide in half.

Shape, let rise, and bake dough as suggested below; or turn dough over in a well-greased bowl, cover, and refrigerate for as long as 24 hours. Makes 2 butter-topped loaves (cut 18 slices per loaf) or 48 crescent rolls.

Per slice: 4 grams protein, 17 grams carbohydrate, 21 milligrams cholesterol, 104 calories.

Per crescent roll: 3 grams protein, 14 grams carbohydrate, 19 milligrams cholesterol, 94 calories.

Herb Cheese Dough. Prepare dough as directed above, but when

Mushrooms and cashews inside, flavorful whole wheat on the outside —they're Chinese Steamed Buns (recipe on page 76), an excellent choice to serve with Savory Vegetables & Tofu (recipe on page 61) or any stir-fried dish.

you add eggs, also add 1 teaspoon *each* **oregano** and **basil leaves**; ½ teaspoon *each* **savory leaves, thyme leaves,** and **garlic powder**; ¼ teaspoon **pepper**; and ¼ cup *each* **instant toasted onion** and grated **Parmesan cheese**.

Butter-topped Loaves. Divide dough (wheat or herb) in half and shape each half into a smooth loaf. Place in 2 greased 5 by 9-inch loaf pans. Cover and let rise in a warm place until dough has risen 1 inch above pan rims (about 1½ hours).

Butter a razor blade or sharp knife and make a ¼-inch-deep slash lengthwise down tops of loaves. Drizzle each slash with 1 tablespoon melted **butter** or margarine. Bake in a 375° oven for 45 minutes or until browned. Turn out onto a rack.

Crescent Rolls. Divide dough (wheat or herb) into 4 equal portions; shape each into a smooth ball. On a floured board, roll out each ball into a 12-inch circle, brush with 1 tablespoon melted **butter** or margarine, and cut into 12 equal wedges. Starting from the wide end, roll up each wedge toward the point. Place rolls, points down, 2 inches apart on well-greased baking sheets. Curve each roll slightly and brush lightly with 1 **egg white** beaten with 1 tablespoon **water**. Sprinkle lightly with **sesame seeds,** if desired. Cover and let rise in a warm place until very puffy (about 45 minutes).

Bake in a 400° oven for about 15 minutes or until golden. Cool on wire racks.

Honey-Wheat Buns

Caution! Sandwich construction site ahead. You can build a sandwich really worth munching if you have these buns and your favorite sandwich fixings. The buns are made with cottage cheese, so they have an extra boost of

protein. For an unusual sandwich filling, try chopped, cooked artichoke hearts, tomato slices, and sprouts.

1 cup *each* bulgur wheat and boiling water

2 packages active dry yeast

½ cup warm water (about 110°)

⅓ cup honey

2 tablespoons salad oil

1 tablespoon salt

1½ cups small curd cottage cheese

3 eggs

About 6½ cups whole wheat flour

In a large bowl, stir together bulgur and boiling water; let cool to lukewarm. Meanwhile, dissolve yeast in the warm water and stir into bulgur. Add honey, oil, salt, cottage cheese, and eggs; mix well. Gradually add 3 cups of the flour, beating well after each addition.

With a heavy-duty mixer or wooden spoon, beat in enough of the remaining flour (about 3 cups) to form a stiff dough. Turn dough out onto a floured board and knead briefly as you shape dough into a smooth ball; dough will be a little sticky. Turn dough over in a greased bowl, cover, and let rise in a warm place until doubled (about 1½ hours).

Punch down dough, turn out onto a floured board, and divide into 20 equal pieces. Shape each piece into a smooth ball by kneading briefly on floured board; dough will still be a little sticky.

Place balls about 2 inches apart on greased baking sheets and flatten slightly. Cover lightly and let stand in a warm place until puffy and almost doubled (about 45 minutes).

Bake buns in a 375° oven until lightly browned (about 12 to 15 minutes). Let cool on wire racks, then package airtight or freeze to store. Makes 20 buns.

Per bun: 10 grams protein, 40 grams carbohydrate, 51 milligrams cholesterol, 230 calories.

Maple-Molasses Bread

A slice of this round loaf when it's fresh from the oven is pure bliss; toasted, it's even better.

> 2 tablespoons sugar
> 1½ cups warm water (about 110°)
> 1 package active dry yeast
> ⅓ cup maple or maple-flavored syrup
> ⅓ cup *each* molasses (dark or light) and salad oil
> 1 teaspoon salt
> 3½ cups all-purpose flour
> About 4 cups whole wheat flour
> 1 cup raisins
> Salad oil
> 1 egg white beaten with 1 teaspoon water

In a large bowl, dissolve sugar in the warm water. Stir in yeast and let stand for 5 minutes. Blend in maple syrup, molasses, oil, and salt. Beat in all-purpose flour, 1 cup at a time, then beat until dough pulls away from bowl in stretchy strands (about 10 to 15 minutes at medium speed if using electric mixer). With a heavy-duty mixer or wooden spoon, gradually beat in 3 cups of the whole wheat flour.

Turn dough out on a floured board and knead until smooth and elastic (10 to 15 minutes), adding more whole wheat flour as needed to prevent sticking. Gradually knead in raisins during the last 5 minutes of kneading time. Turn dough over in a greased bowl; cover and let rise in a warm place until doubled (about 2 hours).

Punch dough down and turn onto a lightly floured board. Divide dough in half; shape each half into a smooth ball and place in a greased 8-inch pie pan. Lightly brush tops with salad oil; cover and let rise in a warm place until doubled (45 minutes to 1 hour).

Brush egg white mixture over loaves. Bake in a 375° oven for 30 minutes or until loaves are dark golden and sound hollow when tapped. Cool in pan for 10 minutes, then turn out onto racks to cool completely. Makes 2 loaves; cut 18 slices per loaf.

Per slice: 3 grams protein, 26 grams carbohydrate, no cholesterol, 136 calories.

Chinese Steamed Buns

(Pictured on page 74)

The buns are flavorful whole wheat. The filling is a marvelous mixture of mushrooms, cashews, and other goodies prepared with fresh ginger, a little garlic, and soy sauce. You can steam them or bake them; either way, they're superb.

> 1 package active dry yeast
> 1 cup warm water (about 110°)
> 1 tablespoon sugar
> 2 tablespoons salad oil
> 1 teaspoon salt
> About 2¾ cups whole wheat flour
> Mushroom-Cashew Filling (recipe follows)
> 1 tablespoon butter or margarine (for baked buns)

In a large bowl, dissolve yeast in the warm water; blend in sugar, oil, and salt. Let stand until bubbly (about 15 minutes). Add flour and mix until dough holds together. Place dough on a lightly floured board and knead until smooth and elastic (about 8 to 10 minutes). Turn dough over in a greased bowl; cover and let rise in a warm place until doubled (about 1 hour).

Meanwhile prepare mushroom-cashew filling; let cool and set aside.

Turn dough out onto a lightly floured board and knead for 1 minute. Cut dough into 12 equal pieces.

Roll each piece into a round about 4½ inches in diameter. Press outside edge of round to make it slightly thinner than the rest of the dough. Place about 2 tablespoons filling in center of each round. Pull edges of dough up around filling and twist to seal.

For steamed buns, place each bun, twisted side down, on a 2-inch square of foil and place on a cooky sheet. Cover and let rise in a warm place until puffy and light (about 30 minutes). Set with foil, in a single layer in a steamer over boiling water. Cover and steam for 15 minutes. Serve warm; or let cool, then wrap and refrigerate or freeze. To reheat, steam buns until hot (about 5 to 10 minutes).

For baked buns, place buns about 2 inches apart on a greased cooky sheet. Cover and let rise in a warm place until puffy and light (about 30 minutes). Melt butter; brush over tops. Bake in a 350° oven until bottoms of buns turn golden brown (about 15 minutes). Makes 12 buns.

Per steamed bun: 6 grams protein, 26 grams carbohydrate, no cholesterol, 195 calories.

Per baked bun: 6 grams protein, 26 grams carbohydrate, 3 milligrams cholesterol, 200 calories.

Mushroom-Cashew Filling. Prepare the following: ¼ pound **mushrooms,** chopped; 1 small **onion,** chopped; 1 clove **garlic,** minced or pressed; 1 teaspoon minced **fresh ginger;** ½ cup coarsely chopped **bamboo shoots;** ¾ cup coarsely chopped **cashews;** and 2 **green onions,** including tops, thinly sliced. In a bowl, combine 3 tablespoons **soy sauce,** 1 tablespoon **dry sherry,** 1 teaspoon **sugar,** ¼ cup **water,** and 1 tablespoon **cornstarch.**

Heat 1 tablespoon **salad oil** in a wide frying pan over high heat. Add mushrooms, onion, garlic, and ginger and stir-fry for 3 minutes. Add bamboo shoots, cashews, and green onions and cook for 2 minutes. Pour in soy mixture and cook, stirring, until sauce bubbles and thickens. Stir in 1 teaspoon **sesame oil.** Remove pan from heat; cool.

Anadama Bread

Legend has it that Anna's disgruntled New England husband muttered "Anna, damn her" as he recombined the unimaginative ingredients of Anna's dinner—cornmeal and molasses—to make this bread. We say, "Anna, bless her," and add bananas and dates to make a bread that's just perfect when you spread it with cream cheese.

  1½ cups whole wheat flour
  ¾ cup cornmeal
  ¾ teaspoon salt
  ½ teaspoon baking soda
  1 package active dry yeast
  2½ tablespoons salad oil
  ¼ cup light molasses
  1 cup plus 2 tablespoons very warm water (120° to 130°)
  About 3 cups all-purpose flour
  ½ cup mashed ripe banana
  1 cup diced pitted dates
  About 1 teaspoon cornmeal

In a large bowl, mix together whole wheat flour, the ¾ cup cornmeal, salt, baking soda, and yeast. Stir in oil, molasses, and the warm water; beat (at medium speed for 2 minutes if using electric mixer). Add ¼ cup of the all-purpose flour and beat (at high speed for 2 minutes with electric mixer). With a heavy duty mixer or wooden spoon, stir in the banana and about 2½ cups of the all-purpose flour—enough to make a stiff dough.

Turn dough out onto a floured board and knead until smooth, adding all-purpose flour as necessary to prevent sticking. Knead dates into dough, a portion at a time. Turn dough over in a greased bowl. Cover and let rise in a warm place until doubled (about 1½ hours).

Grease a 9-inch pie pan and sprinkle with the 1 teaspoon cornmeal. Punch down dough, knead a few times, then shape into a smooth ball. Place in pie pan; cover and let rise in a warm place until almost doubled (about 45 minutes).

Bake in a 375° oven until browned (35 to 40 minutes). Turn out onto a rack to cool. Makes 1 large loaf; cut in 20 slices.

Per slice: 4 grams protein, 35 grams carbohydrate, no cholesterol, 173 calories.

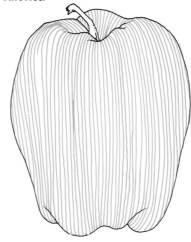

Casserole Cheese Bread

Baked in one-cup custard or soufflé dishes, this recipe turns out six miniature loaves. Both Cheddar and Parmesan cheeses go into the dough, then more Cheddar is sprinkled on top to give each loaf a golden crown.

  1 package active dry yeast
  ¼ cup warm water (about 110°)
  ¾ cup milk
  1 tablespoon butter or margarine
  1 tablespoon instant minced onion
  2 tablespoons sugar
  1 teaspoon salt
  1 egg
  About 1¼ cups all-purpose flour
  About 1⅛ cups whole wheat flour
  1½ cups (6 oz.) shredded Cheddar cheese
  ⅓ cup grated Parmesan cheese

In a bowl, sprinkle yeast over the warm water. In a pan over medium heat, combine milk, butter, onion, and sugar. Heat to 110°. Blend into yeast mixture. Add salt and egg and mix well. Gradually beat in 1⅛ cups of the all-purpose flour and all of the whole wheat flour, adding a little more all-purpose flour if necessary to make a stiff, sticky dough. Stir in 1 cup of the Cheddar cheese and all the Parmesan cheese. Cover and let rise in a warm place until almost doubled (about 1 hour).

Stir dough down and divide equally among 6 greased 1-cup baking dishes (such as custard or soufflé dishes). Cover and let rise in a warm place until almost doubled (20 to 30 minutes). Sprinkle tops with the remaining ½ cup Cheddar cheese. Bake in a 350° oven until richly browned (about 30 minutes). Remove bread from dishes and cool. Makes 6 servings.

Per serving: 17 grams protein, 42 grams carbohydrate, 85 milligrams cholesterol, 369 calories.

Golden Swiss Cheese Loaves

There's so much cheese in this bread that a slice of it, toasted, tastes like a grilled cheese sandwich. It's a natural partner for soups and salads and makes a wonderful sandwich with avocado, sprouts, and tomato.

  2 packages active dry yeast
  1½ cups warm water (about 110°)
  2 tablespoons sugar
  4 tablespoons butter or margarine, melted and cooled
  1 teaspoon liquid hot pepper seasoning
  ¼ cup wheat germ
  About 4½ to 5 cups all-purpose flour
  ¾ cup shredded Swiss cheese
  ⅓ cup grated Parmesan cheese
  Melted butter or margarine

(Continued on next page)

In a large bowl, dissolve yeast in the warm water. Stir in sugar, the 4 tablespoons melted butter, hot pepper seasoning, wheat germ, and 2 cups of the flour. Beat, scraping bowl often for 4 minutes (at medium speed if using electric mixer). Add 1 more cup of the flour and beat (for 4 more minutes at high speed with electric mixer).

With a heavy-duty mixer or wooden spoon, beat in enough of the remaining flour (about 1½ cups) to form a soft dough that is not too sticky to knead. Turn out onto a floured board and knead until smooth, adding remaining flour as needed to prevent sticking. Turn dough over in a greased bowl; cover and let rise in a warm place until doubled (about 1½ hours).

Punch down dough and gradually knead in Swiss cheese and all but about 2 tablespoons of the Parmesan cheese. Divide dough in half; shape each half into a smooth loaf and place in a greased 4 by 8-inch loaf pan. Cover and let rise in a warm place until loaves have risen slightly above pan rims (about 2 hours).

Brush lightly with melted butter and sprinkle with remaining Parmesan cheese. Bake in a 350° oven until loaves are browned and sound hollow when tapped (30 to 35 minutes). Turn out onto racks to cool completely. Makes 2 loaves; cut 16 slices per loaf.

Per slice: 3 grams protein, 15 grams carbohydrate, 8 milligrams cholesterol, 97 calories.

Graham Yogurt Bread

Here is a nutritious, even-textured bread that bakes in three 1-pound vegetable or fruit cans (*not* coffee cans). Tightly wrapped and stored in the refrigerator, these loaves stay fresh for about 5 days. This bread is especially good lightly toasted.

2 cups graham flour or whole wheat flour
½ cup all-purpose flour
2 teaspoons baking soda
1 teaspoon salt
2 cups plain yogurt
½ cup molasses (dark or light)
1 cup raisins
½ cup chopped walnuts

Remove one end from each of three 1-pound cans (see introduction above); rinse, dry, and grease cans well. In a large bowl, stir together graham flour, all-purpose flour, baking soda, and salt until thoroughly blended. Stir in yogurt, molasses, raisins, and walnuts; mix well. Distribute batter evenly among cans.

Bake in a 350° oven for about 1 hour or until a wooden skewer inserted in center of loaves comes out clean. Cool in cans for about 10 minutes; then turn out and stand loaves upright on a rack to cool completely. Makes 3 small loaves; cut 6 slices per loaf.

Per slice: 4 grams protein, 26 grams carbohydrate, 2 milligrams cholesterol, 137 calories.

Quick Corn Bread

(Pictured on page 50)

High and light, moist and tender, with a hint of sweetness. . . this corn bread can be stirred together in minutes when you want a hot bread to serve with dinner.

1 cup *each* baking mix (biscuit mix) and yellow cornmeal
3 teaspoons baking powder
2 eggs
1 cup milk
⅓ cup honey
4 tablespoons butter or margarine, melted and cooled

In a large bowl, stir together baking mix, cornmeal, and baking pow-

der. In a small bowl, beat eggs lightly; stir in milk, honey, and butter. Pour egg mixture into dry ingredients and mix just until moistened.

Turn batter into a well-greased 8-inch square or round baking pan. Bake in a 400° oven for 25 to 30 minutes or until a wood skewer inserted in center comes out clean. Cut into squares or wedges and serve warm. Makes 9 servings.

Per serving: 5 grams protein, 31 grams carbohydrate, 76 milligrams cholesterol, 224 calories.

Apple Brown Bread

Bits of fresh apple dot this wholesome molasses-flavored brown bread. A moist loaf, it slices more easily the day after it's baked.

½ cup (¼ lb.) butter or margarine
½ cup firmly packed brown sugar
1 egg
½ cup dark molasses
2 cups all-purpose flour
1½ cups graham flour or whole wheat flour
½ cup wheat germ
2 teaspoons baking soda
1 teaspoon *each* baking powder and salt
2 cups buttermilk
2 cups finely chopped, unpeeled, tart apples
1 cup chopped walnuts

In a large bowl, beat together butter and brown sugar until light and

Daisy-bright start in the morning. . . light-textured Oatmeal Pancakes with Blueberry Sauce (recipe on page 84) contain rolled oats and wheat germ; Orange Froth (recipe on page 83) combines milk, eggs, and orange juice for high nutrition.

creamy. Beat in egg; then stir in molasses until blended. In another bowl, stir together all-purpose flour, graham flour, wheat germ, baking soda, baking powder, and salt until thoroughly blended.

Add dry ingredients alternately with buttermilk to creamed mixture; after each addition mix just until blended. Stir in apples and nuts. Spoon batter into 2 greased and flour-dusted 4 by 8-inch loaf pans.

Bake in a 350° oven for about 1½ hours or until bread begins to pull away from sides of pans and a wooden skewer inserted in center comes out clean. Let cool in pans for 10 minutes; then turn out onto a rack to cool completely. Makes 2 loaves; cut 16 slices per loaf.

Per slice: 3 grams protein, 20 grams carbohydrate, 17 milligrams cholesterol, 141 calories.

Cottage Cheese Muffins

Cottage cheese adds moistness to these whole grain muffins; cornmeal gives them an intriguingly crunchy texture.

1½ **cups all-purpose flour**
½ **cup buckwheat or whole wheat flour**
1 **cup yellow cornmeal**
4½ **teaspoons baking powder**
¼ **teaspoon salt**
3 **tablespoons sugar**
2 **eggs**
1 **cup *each* small curd cottage cheese and buttermilk**
⅓ **cup salad oil**

In a large bowl, combine all-purpose flour, buckwheat flour, cornmeal, baking powder, salt, and sugar; mix well. In a small bowl, beat eggs lightly; mix in cottage cheese, buttermilk, and oil. Make a well in center of flour mixture and add liquid ingredients all at once.

Stir with a fork just enough to blend ingredients.

Spoon into well-greased 2 to 3-inch muffin cups, filling them about two-thirds full. Bake in a 400° oven until golden brown (about 20 minutes). Turn out of pans onto a rack. Makes 2 dozen muffins.

Per muffin: 4 grams protein, 14 grams carbohydrate, 23 milligrams cholesterol, 107 calories.

Cheddar Cheese Popovers

A big crisp popover, hot from the oven, makes the perfect partner to a bowl of soup or a main-dish salad for lunch or supper.

1 **cup all-purpose flour**
½ **teaspoon Mexican seasoning (or ¼ teaspoon chili powder and a dash *each* ground cumin, garlic powder, and oregano leaves)**
¼ **teaspoon garlic salt**
1 **tablespoon melted butter or margarine**
1 **cup milk**
3 **eggs**
1 **cup (4 oz.) shredded sharp Cheddar cheese**
¼ **cup finely chopped ripe olives**

Preheat oven to 375°.

In a bowl, combine flour, Mexican seasoning, and garlic salt. Add butter, milk, and eggs and beat,

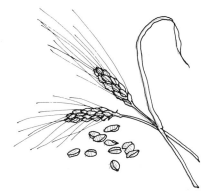

scraping bowl frequently, until very smooth (about 2½ minutes at medium-high speed if using electric mixer). Beat in cheese and olives.

Evenly distribute batter in 12 well-greased ½-cup-size containers (muffin tins or ovenproof glass custard cups). Bake on center rack in the preheated 375° oven for 45 to 50 minutes or until well browned and firm to touch. Remove from containers and serve hot.

If you like popovers to be especially dry, loosen from pan but leave sitting at an angle in cups; prick popovers' sides with a skewer and let stand in the turned-off oven with door slightly ajar for 8 to 10 minutes. Makes 12 popovers.

Per popover: 6 grams protein, 9 grams carbohydrate, 78 milligrams cholesterol, 122 calories.

Sesame Swirls

If your family favors biscuits, you might want to serve these easy-to-make dinner rolls filled with toasted sesame seeds.

2 **tablespoons butter or margarine**
½ **cup sesame seeds**
2½ **cups all-purpose flour**
2½ **teaspoons baking powder**
1 **teaspoon salt**
½ **cup butter or margarine**
1 **cup sour cream**
½ **cup milk**
1 **egg, lightly beaten**

Melt the 2 tablespoons butter in a small frying pan over medium heat. Add sesame seeds and cook, stirring, until toasted; set aside to cool.

In a bowl, stir together flour, baking powder, and salt until well blended. With a pastry blender or 2 knives, cut the ½ cup butter into flour mixture until it resembles coarse crumbs. In a separate bowl, stir together sour cream and milk. Add to flour mixture, blending gently. Turn out on a lightly floured board and knead gently about 5 times.

Roll out dough to a rectangle about 15 inches long, 12 inches wide, and ¼ inch thick. Brush with half the beaten egg, then spread with toasted sesame seeds. Starting with long side, roll up jelly-roll fashion; pinch edge to seal. Cut roll with a floured knife into 1-inch slices and place slices, cut side up, on a lightly greased baking sheet. Brush slices with remaining egg.

Bake in a 425° oven for about 15 minutes or until lightly browned. Makes 16 biscuits.

Per biscuit: 4 grams protein, 17 grams carbohydrate, 46 milligrams cholesterol, 199 calories.

Whole Wheat Tortillas

These versatile flat breads can be served hot and soft from the griddle, deep-fried until crisp, or used in Mexican cookery.

2 cups whole wheat flour
½ teaspoon salt
4 tablespoons butter or margarine
½ cup lukewarm water
All-purpose flour

Combine whole wheat flour and salt in a mixing bowl. With a pastry blender or 2 knives, cut butter into flour mixture until it resembles fine crumbs. Add water gradually, tossing with a fork to mix. Turn out onto a board and knead for a minute or two until well mixed. Shape into a ball; cover and let rest for 15 minutes.

Divide and shape dough into 8 balls for 9-inch tortillas, 12 balls for 6-inch tortillas. Keep balls covered to prevent them from drying out. On a board lightly dusted with all-purpose flour, roll out one ball at a time as thin as possible. As each tortilla is shaped, place in a preheated ungreased heavy frying pan or on a griddle over medium-high heat. Almost immediately, blisters should appear. Use a wide spatula to press gently but firmly all over the top. Blisters will form over most of surface as you press. Turn and cook to brown the other side.

Stack cooked tortillas in a tightly covered dish or wrap tightly in foil to keep them soft. Serve while still warm; or cool tortillas, wrap airtight, and refrigerate.

To reheat tortillas, wrap with foil, and heat in a 350° oven for 15 minutes. Makes 8 large tortillas or 12 small tortillas.

Per large tortilla: 4 grams protein, 21 grams carbohydrate, 18 milligrams cholesterol, 150 calories.

Chapaties

Four minutes is all it takes to cook this simple wheat-flavored bread that accompanies almost every meal in India. Mild in flavor and slightly chewy, chapaties are a delicious balance to hot spicy foods, hearty soups, and crisp salads.

2 cups whole wheat flour
1 teaspoon salt
About ⅔ cup warm water

In a bowl, stir together flour and salt. With a fork, gradually stir in water until a crumbly dough forms. With your hands, work dough until it holds together. Add a few more drops water, if needed. On a floured board, knead dough until it is smooth but still sticky (about 3 minutes). Wrap airtight in plastic wrap and let rest for 30 minutes.

Divide and shape dough into 16 smooth balls and flatten each ball with your hand. On a floured board, roll each flattened ball into a circle about 5 inches in diameter. Stack circles, separated by sheets of wax paper. If made ahead, seal in a plastic bag, and refrigerate until next day.

Preheat an ungreased heavy frying pan or griddle over medium-low heat. Place rounds of dough in pan. After about 1 minute, top surface of dough will darken slightly. Use a wide spatula to press directly on top of dough; blisters will gradually appear on top. When bottom browns lightly (about 2 minutes), turn bread over and bake until lightly browned on other side (about 2 minutes more). Serve hot. Makes 16 chapaties.

Per chapatie: 2 grams protein, 11 grams carbohydrate, no cholesterol, 50 calories.

Puris

(Pictured on page 63)

These little Indian breads start out like chapaties, but instead of baking them on a griddle, you deep-fry them in hot oil. Each round puffs up like a balloon and becomes crisp.

Chapatie dough (preceding recipe)
Salad oil

Prepare chapatie dough. Roll out pieces of dough on board lightly rubbed with salad oil rather than flour.

In a deep pan at least 6 inches in diameter, pour salad oil to a depth of 1½ inches and heat to 350° on a deep-frying thermometer. Place one puri at a time in the hot oil. In a few seconds it will bubble up to the surface and start to inflate unevenly like a balloon. With a slotted spoon, very gently press puri against side or bottom of pan so it will inflate completely. Turn over and continue cooking until golden brown (about 1 minute). Remove and drain on paper towels. Serve warm. Makes 16 puris.

Per puri: 2 grams protein, 11 grams carbohydrate, no cholesterol, 98 calories.

Up at 5 a.m. Deep knee bends while feeding cat. Milk goat. Grind wheat. Make four-course breakfast.

What? That's not your morning routine? Yours is a quick cup of coffee and a dash for the door? Well, we're not going to mention the early bird, worms, being healthy, wealthy, and wise, or any other of those adages guaranteed to make those who resent mornings even more resentful. We're just going to offer some recipes and breakfast ideas for food so tempting, you'll want to get up in the morning to try them.

On the next four pages you'll find innovative breakfast suggestions, as well as traditional breakfast foods. Most vegetarians are very nutrition conscious and want every calorie to count. They prefer whole grains in their breads, cereals, and pancakes instead of refined flour; and that's what you'll find in our recipes.

Cereal Suggestions

Granola-type cereals give you grains, dried fruit, and nuts in crunchy combination. The next two recipes, sweetened with honey and baked at low temperatures, are delicious with milk, or eaten dry as a snack or portable breakfast. Then we offer a recipe for hot cereal that combines the nutrients of grains, milk, eggs, and fruit in one bowl.

Spiced Fruit Granola. In a large bowl, combine 3½ cups regular or quick-cooking **rolled oats;** 1 cup *each* chopped **walnuts,** shredded **coconut,** and slivered **almonds;** ½ cup *each* **wheat germ** and **sesame seeds;** 1 teaspoon **ground cinnamon;** and ½ teaspoon **ground cloves.** In a small bowl, stir together ¼ cup *each* **salad oil** and **honey,** and 2 tablespoons grated **orange peel.** Pour over oat mixture and stir to coat evenly.

Spread mixture in two large baking pans. Bake, uncovered, in a 200° oven, stirring occasionally, for about 55 minutes or until lightly toasted. Cool completely, then stir in ½ cup *each* **raisins** and chopped **dried apricots.** Cover and store at room temperature. Makes 8 cups.

Per ⅓ cup serving: 5 grams protein, 19 grams carbohydrate, no cholesterol, 204 calories.

Puffed Cereal Granola. In a large bowl, combine 6 ounces (about 13 cups) unsweetened **puffed cereal** (corn, rice, wheat, or millet), 1 cup **sunflower seeds,** and 1 cup *each* coarsely chopped **peanuts** and **cashews.** In a small bowl, stir together 2 tablespoons **vanilla** and ½ cup *each* **honey, water,** and **salad oil.** Pour over cereal mixture and stir to coat evenly.

Spread mixture in two large baking pans. Bake, uncovered, in a 275° oven, stirring occasionally, for about 45 minutes or until golden. Cool completely, then stir in 2 cups chopped **dried apples** and ½ cup chopped **dates,** figs, or pitted prunes. Cover and store at room temperature. Makes 10 cups.

Per ⅓ cup serving: 3 grams protein, 19 grams carbohydrate, no cholesterol, 154 calories.

Hot Cereal with Fruit. In a pan, bring to a boil 1½ cups **water;** 1 cup **rye flakes,** wheat flakes, or rice flakes; and ½ teaspoon **salt.** Cover, reduce heat, and simmer until liquid is absorbed.

Meanwhile, lightly beat 2 **eggs** with ½ cup **milk** and 1 cup **applesauce.** Stir some hot cereal into egg mixture, then return all to pan. Also stir in ½ cup chopped pitted **dates** or dried apricots and ¼ cup toasted **coconut** or sliced almonds. Heat, stirring, until hot. Serve with milk or light cream. Makes 4 servings.

Per serving: 8 grams protein, 41 grams carbohydrate, 131 milligrams cholesterol, 255 calories.

Breakfast Sandwiches

Sandwiches are a slightly unorthodox but delicious substitute for the usual morning fare. Here are several ideas for wake-up sandwiches.

Peanut Honey Crisps. In a bowl, blend 3 tablespoons *each* **peanut butter,** softened **butter** or margarine, and **honey.** Spread evenly on 8 slices toasted **whole wheat bread.** Place side by side on a baking sheet; sprinkle evenly with 2 tablespoons **sesame seeds.** Bake in a 325° oven for 10 minutes; then broil 4 inches from heat until lightly toasted (about 45 seconds). Cut each slice in half. Makes 8 servings.

Per serving: 5 grams protein, 20 grams carbohydrate, 15 milligrams cholesterol, 170 calories.

Grilled Fruit & Cheese Sandwich. For each sandwich, use 2 slices **whole wheat bread** or oatmeal bread, 2 or 3 slices peeled **apple** or pear (cut ¼ inch thick), 2 slices (½ oz. *each*) **Cheddar** or jack cheese, and 1 teaspoon softened **butter** or margarine. Butter one side of each slice of bread. To assemble each sandwich, lay 1 bread slice, buttered side down, on a flat surface and top bread with a slice of cheese; place fruit slices over cheese, cover with another slice of cheese, then top with bread (buttered side up). Bake in heated grill until bread is toasted and cheese is melted. Or cook in a wide frying pan over medium heat, turning as needed, until browned on each side.

Per sandwich: 12 grams protein, 26 grams carbohydrate, 42 milligrams cholesterol, 276 calories.

Apricot-Almond Sandwiches. In a pan, combine 1½ cups **dried apricots** and 1 cup **water.** Cover and simmer for 25 to 30 minutes. If there is still water in pan, uncover and continue cooking until apricots are very soft and most of the water has evaporated. Remove from heat, mash, and stir in ½ to ¼ cup firmly packed **brown sugar.** Then stir in ½ cup chopped **almonds.** Spread 8 slices of **whole wheat bread** or toast with **cream cheese.** Spread apricot-almond filling on top. Makes 8 servings.

Per serving: 6 grams protein, 34 grams carbohydrate, 7 milligrams cholesterol, 209 calories.

Totally Wild Breakfasts

If it's breakfast foods you dislike in the morning, fix what you do like to eat. Where is it written that you can't have a bean burrito for breakfast, or a bowl of hot soup instead of cereal, or even finish up last night's supper?

Or how about breakfast cookies? Half-cup Cookies (page 94) and Chewy Bran Bars (page 94) can be nutrition-packed take-along breakfast treats. The only catch to breakfast cookies is that you have to make them ahead of time. Also, you have to have the willpower not to eat them all at once.

Breakfast Beverages

You can select from a variety of ingredients—milk, yogurt, honey, fruit, juice, eggs—to make nutritious breakfast beverages. So bring out your blender and try one of these quick concoctions.

Strawberry Banana Smoothie. In a blender, whirl until smooth: 1 cup *each* cracked **ice** and **plain yogurt;** 2 cups sliced **strawberries;** 1 **banana,** peeled and sliced; and 2 tablespoons **honey.** Makes 4 servings.

Per serving: 3 grams protein, 25 grams carbohydrate, 6 milligrams cholesterol, 170 calories.

Tropical Smoothie. In a blender, whirl until smooth: 1 cup *each* cracked **ice** and **plain yogurt;** 1 can (8 oz.) **unsweetened crushed pineapple,** drained; 1 **banana,** peeled and sliced; and 1 tablespoon **honey.** Makes 3 servings.

Per serving: 3 grams protein, 27 grams carbohydrate, 6 milligrams cholesterol, 125 calories.

Orange Froth *(pictured on page 79).* In a blender, whirl until smooth: 1 cup *each* **milk** and **water,** ¼ cup **sugar,** 1 teaspoon **vanilla,** 1 can (6 oz.) **frozen orange juice concentrate** (undiluted), 2 **eggs,** and 10 **ice cubes** (crushed). Makes 4 servings.

Per serving: 7 grams protein, 37 grams carbohydrate, 135 milligrams cholesterol, 219 calories.

Strawberry Nog. In a blender, whirl until smooth: 2½ cups sliced **strawberries,** 1 can (6 oz.) **frozen orange juice concentrate** (undiluted), 1½ cups **milk,** ¼ cup **sugar,** 1 teaspoon **vanilla,** 2 **eggs,** and 10 **ice cubes** (crushed). Makes 6 servings.

Per serving: 6 grams protein, 31 grams carbohydrate, 93 milligrams cholesterol, 182 calories.

Cool Apple Nog. In a blender, whirl until smooth: 1 can (12 oz.) **frozen apple juice concentrate** (undiluted), 2 **eggs,** ¼ teaspoon grated **lemon peel,** 1 tablespoon **lemon juice,** ⅛ teaspoon **ground cinnamon,** dash of **ground nutmeg,** ½ cup **milk,** and 10 **ice cubes**

(Continued on next page)

(crushed). Garnish each serving with fresh **mint sprigs.** Makes 4 servings.

Per serving: 5 grams protein, 32 grams carbohydrate, 131 milligrams cholesterol, 179 calories.

Pancakes, Waffles, French Toast & Quick Breads

Airy-light, but packed with nutrition, the following pancakes, waffles, French toast, and quick breads are deliciously persuasive arguments for morning meals.

Oatmeal Pancakes *(pictured on page 79).*
In a bowl, combine 1 cup regular or quick-cooking **rolled oats,** 1 cup **whole wheat flour,** ¼ cup *each* **wheat germ** and **nonfat dry milk powder,** 1 teaspoon **baking soda,** ¼ teaspoon **salt,** and 1 tablespoon **brown sugar.** In another bowl, combine 2 **eggs** (lightly beaten), 2 cups **buttermilk,** and 4 tablespoons **butter** or margarine (melted and cooled). Add all at once to dry ingredients and stir until well blended.

Preheat a griddle or large frying pan over medium heat; grease lightly. Spoon batter, about ¼ cup for each cake, onto griddle; spread batter to make 5-inch circles. Cook until tops are bubbly and appear dry; turn and cook other sides until lightly browned. Makes 16 pancakes.

Per pancake: 3 grams protein, 12 grams carbohydrate, 42 milligrams cholesterol, 185 calories.

Blueberry Sauce *(pictured on page 79).* In a pan, combine ⅓ cup **sugar** and 1 tablespoon **cornstarch;** add 2 cups fresh or frozen and thawed **blueberries,** 2 tablespoons **lemon juice,** and ⅓ cup **water.** Cook over medium heat, stirring, until mixture is thickened. Serve warm or cold over pancakes, waffles, or French toast. Makes 2 cups sauce.

Per 2 tablespoons: .14 grams protein, 7 grams carbohydrate, no cholesterol, 29 calories.

Cottage Cheese Pancakes with Applesauce. Break 3 **eggs** into a blender or food processor. Add 1 cup **small curd cottage cheese** and whirl until blended. Add 2 tablespoons **salad oil,** ¼ cup **whole wheat flour,** and ¼ teaspoon **salt;** whirl until smooth.

Preheat a griddle or large frying pan over medium heat; grease lightly. Pour batter, about ¼ cup for each cake, onto griddle. Cook until tops are bubbly and appear dry; turn and cook other sides until lightly browned.

While pancakes are cooking, heat 1 cup **applesauce** over medium heat. Spoon 2 tablespoons warm sauce over each pancake and sprinkle lightly with **cinnamon.** Makes 8 pancakes.

Per pancake (including applesauce): 6 grams protein, 4 grams carbohydrate, 83 milligrams cholesterol, 71 calories.

Walnut Wheat Griddle Cakes. In a bowl, stir together 1 cup **whole wheat flour,** ⅓ cup **soy flour,** ¾ teaspoon **salt,** and 3 teaspoons **baking powder.** In another bowl, combine 2 **eggs** (lightly beaten), 1¼ cups **milk,** 2 tablespoons **honey,** and ⅓ cup **salad oil.** Pour all at once into flour mixture and stir until smooth. Stir in ½ cup chopped **walnuts.**

Preheat a griddle or large frying pan over medium heat; grease lightly. Pour batter, about ¼ cup for each cake, onto griddle to make 4-inch circles; space them well apart (they spread). Cook until tops are bubbly and appear dry; turn and cook other sides until lightly browned. Makes 1 dozen pancakes.

Per pancake: 5 grams protein, 13 grams carbohydrate, 46 milligrams cholesterol, 153 calories.

Cornmeal Waffles. Separate 2 **eggs.** Place yolks in a large bowl; place whites in a small bowl and reserve. Beat yolks together with 2 cups **buttermilk.** In another bowl, combine 1 cup **whole wheat flour,** ¾ cup **cornmeal,** 2 teaspoons **baking powder,** 1 teaspoon **baking soda,** ½ teaspoon **salt,** 2 tablespoons **sugar,** and ¼ cup **wheat germ.** Gradually add flour mixture to yolk mixture, blending until smooth. Stir in 6 tablespoons **butter** or margarine (melted and cooled).

Beat the reserved egg whites just until stiff, moist peaks form; fold into batter just until blended. Bake waffles in a preheated waffle iron according to manufacturer's directions. Makes 1 dozen 4-inch square waffles.

Per waffle: 5 grams protein, 18 grams carbohydrate, 61 milligrams cholesterol, 155 calories.

Orange Yogurt Waffles.   Separate 4 **eggs.** Place yolks in a large bowl; place whites in a small bowl and reserve. Beat yolks together with 2 cups **plain yogurt,** 1 tablespoon grated **orange peel,** ¼ cup **orange juice,** 2 tablespoons **sugar,** ¼ teaspoon **ground nutmeg,** and 6 tablespoons **butter** or margarine (melted and cooled); beat until blended.

In another bowl, combine 1 cup **all-purpose flour,** ¾ cup **whole wheat flour,** ¼ cup **wheat germ,** 1 teaspoon *each* **baking powder** and **salt,** and 2 teaspoons **baking soda.** Gradually stir flour mixture into yolk mixture just until moistened; do not beat.

Beat the reserved egg whites just until stiff, moist peaks form; fold into batter. Bake waffles in a preheated waffle iron according to manufacturer's directions. Makes 1 dozen 4-inch square waffles.

Per waffle: 6 grams protein, 20 grams carbohydrate, 105 milligrams cholesterol, 182 calories.

Bran Wheat Waffles.   Separate 2 **eggs.** Place yolks in a large bowl; place whites in a small bowl and reserve. Beat yolks together with 1½ cups **milk,** ¼ cup firmly packed **brown sugar,** and ⅓ cup **butter** or margarine (melted and cooled).

In another bowl, combine ⅔ cup *each* **all-purpose flour** and **whole wheat flour,** ¾ cup **unprocessed bran,** 1 tablespoon **baking powder,** and ½ teaspoon **salt.** Gradually add flour mixture to yolk mixture, blending until smooth.

Beat the reserved egg whites just until stiff, moist peaks form; fold into batter just until blended. Bake waffles in a preheated waffle iron according to manufacturer's directions. Makes eight 4-inch waffles.

Per waffle: 6 grams protein, 25 grams carbohydrate, 85 milligrams cholesterol, 195 calories.

Cashew French Toast.   In a blender, place ¾ cup **milk,** ½ cup **cashews,** 3 tablespoons chopped pitted **dates** or moist-pack dried apricots, and a dash of **salt.** Whirl until smooth. Pour into a pie pan.

Dip 3 slices whole wheat or oatmeal **bread,** one at a time, in milk-nut mixture to coat each side. Melt 1 tablespoon **butter** or margarine in a wide frying pan over medium heat. Place

dipped bread in pan and cook until browned on bottoms. Turn and brown other sides. Repeat, with 3 more slices bread and remaining milk-nut mixture, adding more butter to pan as needed. Sprinkle with **powdered sugar** before serving. Makes 6 slices.

Per slice: 6 grams protein, 23 grams carbohydrate, 17 milligrams cholesterol, 203 calories.

Apricot Bran Scones.   In a bowl, stir together 1 cup *each* **all-purpose** and **whole wheat flour,** ¼ cup **sugar,** 4 teaspoons **baking powder,** and 2 cups **bran flake cereal.** With a pastry blender or two knives, cut in 4 tablespoons **butter** or margarine until mixture resembles coarse crumbs. Stir in 2 **eggs** (lightly beaten), ⅓ cup **milk,** and ½ cup chopped moist-pack **dried apricots** or pitted prunes. Turn out onto a floured board and knead about 6 times; divide dough into thirds.

On a greased baking sheet, pat each third into a 5-inch circle about ½ inch thick. With a floured knife, cut each round into 6 wedges (leave wedges in place). Bake in the middle of a 400° oven for 15 to 20 minutes or until lightly browned. Separate wedges before serving. Makes 18 scones.

Per scone: 3 grams protein, 19 grams carbohydrate, 36 milligrams cholesterol, 116 calories.

Gold Surprise Muffins.   In a large bowl, beat together ¼ cup **butter** or margarine and ¼ cup firmly packed **brown sugar** until creamy. Add 2 **eggs** and beat until light and fluffy. Add 1 tablespoon *each* **lemon juice** and **water** and 1 cup lightly packed, finely shredded **carrots.** Stir until well blended.

In another bowl, combine 1 cup all-purpose **flour,** 2 teaspoons **baking powder,** ½ teaspoon **salt,** ¼ teaspoon **ground ginger,** and 2 tablespoons **wheat germ.** Add to carrot mixture. Stir just enough to moisten all the dry ingredients. Spoon batter into greased 2½-inch muffin cups, filling each about ⅔ full.

Bake in a 400° oven for about 18 minutes or until tops spring back when lightly touched. Makes 10 muffins.

Per muffin: 3 grams protein, 17 grams carbohydrate, 65 milligrams cholesterol, 133 calories.

Sweet Endings

As you can see by the big ice cream cone in the middle of this page, sweets and desserts are just as much fun for vegetarians as anyone else. In fact, desserts often play an important nutritional role in vegetarian menus.

We've included a range of desserts in this chapter, from fairly calorie-conscious goodies, such as Ricotta Cheesecake (page 89), to flagrantly rich sweets, such as Marzipan Torte (page 89). You'll find desserts that appeal to the child in you—for instance, Frozen Fruit Yogurts (page 92) and Half-cup Cookies (page 94). And there are desserts that appeal to the sophisticated gourmand side of you—Figs Romanoff (page 91) and Glazed Peach Crêpes (page 90), to name a couple.

Besides old-time favorites like Honey Peach Cobbler (page 91) and Honey Crunch Baked Apples (page 91), we've come up with some new twists on old themes—for instance, cool refreshing Cantaloupe Melba (page 93) and Strawberry Sundae (page 93) made with strawberries in several forms: puréed, sliced, and whole.

Overall, you'll notice that refined sugar makes a limited appearance in these recipes. Fruit and honey are frequently used as sweeteners. Wherever possible, whole wheat flour is used in cookies, cakes, and pies. Fresh fruit is used in abundance for lighter desserts.

We're especially fond of Brandied Ricotta with Fruit (page 91). It's a model of simplicity and superior nutrition. You simply beat ricotta cheese with flavorings and a little sugar, mound it on a platter, and chill. Serving it is the fun part. You surround the ricotta mixture with sliced fresh fruit and simple butter cookies and let your guests make their own fruit-cheese-and-cooky open-faced sandwiches.

If you prefer the even simpler classic finale of cheese and fresh fruit, here are some combinations to consider: pears with Gorgonzola; aged Parmesan with dried figs; pineapple with Monterey jack; peaches with ricotta and a dusting of freshly grated nutmeg; Port du Salut and melon; strawberries with Neufchâtel; grapes with Brie or Camembert; apples with Bel Paese; plums with Cheddar.

For a special fruit and cheese treat, try making your own fresh cheese (directions on page 46) to serve with fresh raspberries, strawberries, blackberries, nectarines, or peaches. Homemade yogurt (page 46) with fruit is another light ending that provides nutritional bonuses and satisfies your sweet tooth as well.

Apple Custard Pie

A pie that's both apple and custard? That's the best of both worlds. The oatmeal crust is also excellent for quiches and fruit pies. For a crunchier filling, you can shred the apples without peeling them.

    Oatmeal Pastry
    (recipe follows)
 4 eggs
 ¾ cup sugar
 4 tablespoons butter or
    margarine, melted and
    cooled
 1 teaspoon vanilla
 ½ teaspoon grated lemon peel
 ¼ teaspoon *each* ground
    cinnamon and nutmeg
    About 3 large Golden
    Delicious apples

Roll out pastry dough and fit into a 9-inch pie pan; flute edge, then set aside.

Lightly beat eggs; add sugar and beat until well blended. Stir in butter, vanilla, lemon peel, cinnamon, and nutmeg.

Peel apples, if desired; coarsely shred apples. You should have about 3 cups lightly packed apples. Stir apples into egg mixture; turn filling into unbaked pastry shell.

Bake pie on the lowest rack of a 425° oven for 10 minutes. Reduce temperature to 350° and bake for 35 to 40 minutes or until a knife inserted in center comes out clean. Cool on a rack for 10 minutes. Serve warm or chilled. Makes 6 servings.

Per serving (including pastry): 8 grams protein, 54 grams carbohydrate, 234 milligrams cholesterol, 471 calories.

Oatmeal Pastry.   In a bowl, mix together 1 cup **all-purpose flour** and ⅓ cup regular or quick-cooking **oats.** With a pastry blender or 2 knives, cut 7 tablespoons cold **butter** or margarine into flour mixture until it resembles coarse crumbs.

With a fork, gradually blend in 2 to 3 tablespoons **cold water.** Press pastry into a ball with your hands. On a floured board, roll out dough ⅛ inch thick. Fit pastry into a 9-inch pie pan (at least 1¼ inches deep).

Pear Crumble Pie

This recipe could be the source of the expression "easy as pie." All you have to do is slice pears and toss them with a little sugar and lemon juice, put them in a pie shell, and add an *easy* spiced topping.

    Whole Wheat Pastry
    (recipe follows)
    Spiced Topping
    (recipe follows)
 5 medium-size pears
 ½ cup sugar
 1 teaspoon grated lemon peel
 3 tablespoons lemon juice

Roll out pastry dough and fit into a 9-inch pie pan; flute edge, then set aside. Prepare topping and set aside.

Peel, halve, core, and slice pears. Lightly toss pear slices with the sugar, lemon peel, and lemon juice. Arrange in unbaked pastry shell. Sprinkle topping over pears.

Bake pie in a 400° oven for 45 minutes or until pears are tender. Serve warm or chilled. Makes 6 servings.

Per serving (including pastry): 6 grams protein, 77 grams carbohydrate, 73 milligrams cholesterol, 552 calories.

Whole Wheat Pastry.   In a bowl, mix together 1 cup **whole wheat flour** and ¼ teaspoon **salt.** With a pastry blender or 2 knives, cut 6 tablespoons **butter** into flour mixture until it resembles coarse crumbs.

With a fork, gradually blend in

just enough **whipping cream** (about 2 tablespoons) to moisten dough. Press pastry into a ball with your hands. On a board floured with **all-purpose flour,** roll out dough ⅛ inch thick. Fit pastry into a 9-inch pie pan (at least 1¼ inches deep).

Spiced Topping.   In a bowl, combine ½ cup *each* **whole wheat flour** and **sugar,** ½ teaspoon *each* **ground ginger** and **ground cinnamon,** ¼ teaspoon **ground mace,** and ¼ cup finely chopped **walnuts.** With a pastry blender or 2 knives, cut ⅓ cup **butter** or margarine into flour mixture until it resembles coarse crumbs.

Carrot Cake

Carrot cake is a "can't miss" dessert, and this chewy, tortelike version is just delicious; yet it's not nearly as rich as traditional carrot cakes.

 2   cups lightly packed,
     shredded raw carrots
 1   cup raisins
 1½ cups *each* sugar and water
 ⅓   cup butter or margarine
 1   cup all-purpose flour
 1½ teaspoons baking soda
 ½   teaspoon *each* salt, ground
     cloves, and ground allspice
 1   teaspoon *each* ground
     nutmeg and ground
     cinnamon
 1   cup whole wheat flour
 1   teaspoon vanilla
 1   cup chopped walnuts

Place carrots, raisins, sugar, water, and butter in a 3-quart pan and bring to a simmer over medium heat; continue to simmer, uncovered, for 5 minutes. Remove from heat and let cool.

In a bowl, sift together all-purpose flour, baking soda, salt, cloves, allspice, nutmeg, and cinnamon; stir in whole wheat flour.

(Continued on next page)

Stir dry ingredients into cooled carrot mixture until flour is moist. Stir in vanilla and walnuts. Spoon into a greased 9-inch square baking pan.

Bake in a 350° oven for 35 minutes or until a wooden pick inserted in center comes out clean. Cool on a rack for 10 minutes. Serve warm or at room temperature. Makes 12 servings.

Per serving: 5 grams protein, 53 grams carbohydrate, 16 milligrams cholesterol, 318 calories.

Sesame Poundcake

(Pictured on page 18)

Sesame seeds and sesame oil richly flavor this moist poundcake. For best flavor, make it a day ahead and refrigerate; but serve at room temperature.

⅓ cup sesame seeds
¾ cup (1½ sticks) butter or margarine, softened
1 cup sugar
4 eggs
2 cups all-purpose flour
½ teaspoon salt
1 teaspoon baking powder
½ cup milk
1 teaspoon *each* vanilla, sesame oil, and grated lemon peel

In a wide frying pan over medium heat, toast sesame seeds, shaking pan frequently, until seeds are golden (about 2 minutes); set aside.

With an electric mixer, beat together butter and sugar until creamy. Add eggs, one at a time, beating well after each addition.

In another bowl, sift together flour, salt, and baking powder; stir in all but 1 tablespoon of the sesame seeds. In a large measuring cup, combine milk, vanilla, sesame oil, and lemon peel. To the butter mixture, add flour mixture alternately with milk mixture, stirring well after each addition; *do not beat or overstir.*

Pour batter into a well-greased and flour-dusted 9-inch tube pan with a removable bottom or a 5 by 9-inch loaf pan. Sprinkle top with the remaining 1 tablespoon seeds.

Bake in a 325° oven for 1 hour or until a wooden pick inserted in center comes out clean. Cool on wire rack. Makes 16 slices.

Per slice: 3 grams protein, 19 grams carbohydrate, 91 milligrams cholesterol, 199 calories.

Carob-Orange Cake

Frankly, we don't think carob tastes like chocolate—it's delicious in its own right, especially when paired with orange flavoring. Here, carob chips go into the batter as well as on top of this moist, single-layer cake.

½ cup (¼ lb.) butter or margarine, softened
1 cup firmly packed brown sugar
2 eggs
1 teaspoon vanilla
1 tablespoon grated orange peel
1 cup *each* whole wheat flour and all-purpose flour
1½ teaspoons baking powder
1 teaspoon baking soda
½ teaspoon salt
1 cup buttermilk
1½ cups (8 oz.) carob baking chips, coarsely chopped
¼ cup chopped walnuts

With an electric mixer, beat together butter and brown sugar until creamy. Add eggs, vanilla, and orange peel; beat until fluffy.

In a separate bowl, mix together whole wheat flour, all-purpose flour, baking powder, baking soda, and salt. Add to butter mixture alternately with the buttermilk, mixing well after each addition. Stir in 1 cup of the chopped carob chips. Mix thoroughly.

Pour batter into a greased 9-inch square baking pan. Combine remaining ½ cup chopped carob chips with nuts and scatter evenly over batter.

Bake in a 350° oven for about 45 minutes or until a wooden pick inserted in center comes out clean. Cool on a rack for 10 minutes. Serve warm or at room temperature. Makes 9 servings.

Per serving: 7 grams protein, 50 grams carbohydrate, 89 milligrams cholesterol, 424 calories.

Whole Wheat Yogurt Poundcake

Just a thin slice of this orange-flavored poundcake will satisfy your sweet tooth. Offer it plain or with frozen yogurt or chilled fruit spooned over each serving.

1 cup (½ lb.) butter or margarine, softened
2 cups firmly packed brown sugar
1 teaspoon *each* grated orange peel and vanilla
3 eggs
2 cups whole wheat flour
¼ cup wheat germ
¼ teaspoon baking soda
½ teaspoon salt
1 cup orange-flavored or plain yogurt
½ cup granola-type cereal

With an electric mixer, beat together butter and sugar until creamy. Beat in orange peel and vanilla. Add eggs, one at a time, beating well after each addition.

In another bowl, stir together whole wheat flour, wheat germ, baking soda, and salt. Add to butter mixture alternately with yogurt, mixing well after each addition.

Pour batter into a greased and flour-dusted 10-inch tube pan with removable bottom. Sprinkle granola over top.

Bake in a 325° oven until a wooden pick inserted in center comes out clean (about 1 hour). Cool in pan on rack. Makes 12 servings.

Per serving: 6 grams protein, 53 grams carbohydrate, 113 milligrams cholesterol, 383 calories.

Yogurt Cheesecake with Dates

This delicious cheesecake is made without the usual eggs or gelatin. You simply combine cream cheese, honey, and yogurt, then chill the mixture in a sesame crumb crust overnight so it will be firm enough to slice.

Sesame Crumb Crust (recipe follows)
1 **large package (8 oz.) cream cheese, softened**
3 **tablespoons honey**
1 **cup plain yogurt**
1 **teaspoon** *each* **vanilla and grated orange peel**
½ **cup** *each* **chopped pitted dates and sliced almonds**

Prepare and bake crust; let cool.

In a bowl, beat cream cheese with honey until fluffy. Gradually mix in yogurt until smooth. Stir in vanilla and orange peel. Turn into prepared crust and spread evenly. Sprinkle dates and almonds evenly over filling. Cover and refrigerate until next day, or freeze.

Serve well chilled. If frozen, thaw for about 20 minutes to serve partially frozen, or allow to thaw

completely in refrigerator. Makes 8 servings.

Per serving: 7 grams protein, 30 grams carbohydrate, 57 milligrams cholesterol, 345 calories.

Sesame Crumb Crust. In a bowl, mix together ¾ cup **dry whole wheat bread crumbs,** ¼ cup **wheat germ,** 2 tablespoons *each* **sugar** and **sesame seeds,** and 5 tablespoons melted **butter** or margarine. Press mixture firmly into bottom and sides of a 9-inch pie pan. Bake in a 375° oven for 8 minutes.

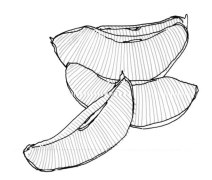

Marzipan Torte

Marzipan is a time-honored confection of ground almonds, sugar, and egg whites. You usually see it around holiday time made into tiny fruits and animals, but here marzipan flavors the filling of a rich torte. Look for cans or tubes of almond paste in supermarkets or gourmet specialty shops.

Marzipan Filling (recipe follows)
1⅓ **cups all-purpose flour**
1 **teaspoon baking powder**
½ **cup (¼ lb.) butter or margarine, softened**
⅓ **cup sugar**
1 **egg**
½ **cup raspberry jam**

Prepare filling and set aside.

In a bowl, stir together flour and baking powder. In a large mixing

bowl, beat together butter and sugar until creamy. Add egg and beat until light and fluffy. Stir in flour mixture and mix well.

Firmly press dough in an even layer in a 9-inch spring-form pan. Spread ¼ cup of the jam over the dough. Spread filling in an even layer over the jam.

Bake in a 350° oven for 50 minutes or until a knife inserted in center comes out clean. Spread remaining ¼ cup jam over the top. Serve chilled. Makes 16 servings.

Per serving: 5 grams protein, 30 grams carbohydrate, 83 milligrams cholesterol, 315 calories.

Marzipan Filling. In a mixing bowl, beat together ½ cup (¼ lb.) softened **butter** or margarine and ⅔ cup **sugar** until creamy. Add 1 can (8 oz.) **almond paste** and ½ teaspoon **almond extract** and beat until smooth. Beat in 2 **eggs,** one at a time, until well blended.

Ricotta Cheesecake

Here's a splendid cheesecake that doesn't have too many calories. For a simpler version with even fewer calories, eliminate the crust —just coat the buttered pan with wheat germ.

Nutty Crumb Crust (recipe follows), or 2 teaspoons butter or margarine and ¼ cup toasted wheat germ
3 **eggs**
3 **cups (1½ pounds) ricotta cheese**
⅔ **cup sugar**
⅓ **cup** *each* **sour cream and cornstarch**
1 **teaspoon** *each* **baking powder and vanilla**
3 **tablespoons butter or margarine, melted and cooled**
2 **teaspoons grated lemon peel**
2 **cups whole strawberries**

(Continued on next page)

Prepare and bake crust. Or spread the 2 teaspoons butter over bottom and sides of a 9-inch cake pan with removable bottom, then sprinkle with wheat germ.

In a blender or food processor, whirl eggs, cheese, sugar, and sour cream until smooth. Blend cornstarch and baking powder; add to cheese mixture with vanilla, butter, and lemon peel. Whirl mixture until well blended. (Or use an electric mixer to prepare filling.) Turn filling into prepared pan.

Bake in a 325° oven for 55 to 60 minutes or until a knife inserted in center comes out clean. Cool on a rack; cover and refrigerate. Garnish each slice with a few strawberries. Makes 12 servings.

Per serving (with Nutty Crumb Crust): 10 grams protein, 29 grams carbohydrate, 105 milligrams cholesterol, 297 calories.

Per serving (with Wheat Germ Crust): 9 grams protein, 21 grams carbohydrate, 95 milligrams cholesterol, 216 calories.

Nutty Crumb Crust. Blend together 1¼ cups finely crushed **graham cracker crumbs,** ¼ cup *each* finely minced **almonds** and melted **butter** or margarine, and 2 tablespoons **sugar.** Press evenly into bottom and sides of a 9-inch cake pan with removable bottom. Bake in a 325° oven for 8 minutes; cool.

Glazed Peach Crêpes

Sliced peaches accented with lemon, nutmeg, and brandy are cooked until tender, then used as a filling and topping for tender whole wheat crêpes. If you use frozen peaches, look for bags of slices that are unsweetened and individually frozen.

As a variation, you could use sliced apples, nectarines, apricots, or pears in place of the peaches.

8 **Whole Wheat Crêpes (page 56)**
2 **tablespoons butter or margarine**
6 **medium-size peaches, peeled and cut in ½-inch-thick slices, or 6 cups unsweetened frozen peach slices, partially defrosted**
1 **teaspoon grated lemon peel**
1 **tablespoon lemon juice**
⅛ **teaspoon ground nutmeg**
½ **cup sugar**
2 **tablespoons brandy**
½ **cup sour cream**

Prepare crêpes and set aside.

Melt butter in a wide frying pan over medium heat. Add peaches, lemon peel, lemon juice, and nutmeg. Cook, gently turning occasionally with a wide spatula, until peaches begin to soften (about 7 minutes). Sprinkle in sugar and cook, stirring gently, for 2 minutes longer. Warm brandy in a small pan, ignite (*not* beneath an exhaust fan or flammable items), then spoon flaming liquid over peaches. Continue cooking until liquid is thickened. Remove from heat and cool slightly.

To assemble, spoon 3 tablespoons filling across lower third of each crêpe and roll to enclose. Place filled crêpes, seam side down, in a lightly buttered baking dish. Spoon remaining filling over top.

Cover and bake in a 325° oven for 25 minutes or until crêpes are heated through. Top each crêpe with a spoonful of sour cream before serving. Makes 8 crêpes.

Per crêpe: 4 grams protein, 29 grams carbohydrate, 65 milligrams cholesterol, 204 calories.

Lemon Yogurt Sponge Torte

Your guests will know they're special when you serve this tangy light torte. It has a layer of delicate cake, a filling of lemon yogurt, another layer of cake, then a topping of whipped cream and coconut.

1 **cup shredded coconut**
4 **eggs, separated**
¾ **cup sugar**
1½ **tablespoons lemon juice**
1 **teaspoon baking powder**
½ **teaspoon grated lemon peel**
½ **cup all-purpose flour**
2 **cups lemon-flavored yogurt**
¾ **cup whipping cream**
1 **tablespoon sugar**
Lemon slices for garnish

Spread coconut on a large baking sheet and bake in a 350° oven for 4 minutes or until golden. Lightly grease a 10 by 15-inch jelly roll pan. Line pan with wax paper; grease the paper.

In a small bowl, beat together egg yolks, ½ cup of the sugar, lemon juice, and baking powder until thick and lemon-colored. Stir in lemon peel and ½ cup of the coconut.

In a large bowl, beat egg whites until soft peaks form. Gradually beat in the remaining ¼ cup sugar until stiff peaks form. Gently fold egg yolk mixture and flour into beaten whites until blended. Pour into prepared pan, spreading evenly. Bake in a 375° oven for 10 to 12 minutes or until top springs back when lightly touched.

Place a piece of wax paper on a large rack (or two smaller racks). Invert cake on rack and peel off paper used in baking; cool.

Cut cake into two layers. Place one layer on a serving platter and spread with yogurt. Set remaining cake layer on yogurt. Whip cream just until stiff; flavor with the 1 tablespoon sugar. Spread whipped cream over top of cake and sprinkle with the remaining ½ cup coconut. Garnish with lemon slices. Chill for at least 2 hours or overnight. Makes 9 servings.

Per serving: 7 grams protein, 37 grams carbohydrate, 136 milligrams cholesterol, 304 calories.

Figs Romanoff

Fresh figs folded into a mixture of ice cream and whipped cream, then garnished with grated chocolate is a sophisticated sweet concoction.

- **2 pounds fresh figs**
- **2 tablespoons curaçao or orange juice**
- **1 pint vanilla ice cream**
- **½ pint (1 cup) whipping cream**
- **1 tablespoon sugar**
- **¼ cup grated sweet chocolate**

Peel figs, if desired, and cut in halves; arrange in a shallow bowl and sprinkle with curaçao. Cover and chill.

About 10 minutes before serving, remove ice cream from freezer to soften. Whip cream until thick and sweeten with sugar. Fold ice cream into whipped cream. Fold in figs. Spoon into small dessert bowls or goblets. Sprinkle chocolate over each serving. Makes 8 servings.

Per serving: 4 grams protein, 37 grams carbohydrate, 46 milligrams cholesterol, 312 calories.

Honey Peach Cobbler

Here's a homey dessert of peaches baked with a topping of whole wheat and honey. We think it's best served warm with vanilla ice cream.

- **6 medium-size peaches, peeled, and cut in ½-inch-thick slices, or 6 cups unsweetened frozen peach slices, partially defrosted**
- **2 tablespoons *each* cornstarch and water**
- **3 tablespoons lemon juice**
- **½ cup honey**
  Whole Wheat & Honey Topping (recipe follows)
- **1 pint vanilla ice cream**

Place peaches in a shallow 3-quart baking dish. In a bowl, mix cornstarch and water. Add lemon juice and honey; stir until blended, then stir into peaches.

Prepare topping as directed and drop by spoonfuls onto fruit mixture. Bake in a 400° oven for 30 to 35 minutes or until well browned. Serve warm or cool, and accompany with ice cream. Makes 8 servings.

Per serving (including ice cream): 6 grams protein, 64 grams carbohydrate, 33 milligrams cholesterol, 348 calories.

Whole Wheat & Honey Topping. In a bowl, stir together 1¼ cups **whole wheat flour,** 2 teaspoons **baking powder,** ½ teaspoon *each* **salt** and **ground cinnamon,** and ¼ teaspoon **ground nutmeg.** With a pastry blender or 2 knives, cut 4 tablespoons cold **butter** or margarine into flour mixture until it resembles coarse crumbs. Combine ½ cup **milk** and ¼ cup **honey;** stir into flour mixture just until blended.

Honey Crunch Baked Apples

Warm or cool, these granola-filled baked apples are delicious topped with cream. Choose a good baking apple such as Rome Beauty, Pippin, or Golden Delicious.

- **6 large baking apples**
- **⅓ cup *each* granola-type cereal (page 82 or purchased) and chopped dates**
- **¼ cup chopped walnuts or almonds**
- **½ teaspoon ground cinnamon**
- **¼ teaspoon ground nutmeg**
- **2 teaspoons lemon juice**
- **⅓ cup honey**
- **3 tablespoons butter or margarine, melted**
- **¾ cup apple juice or water**
- **1 cup half-and-half (light cream)**

Peel apples, if desired, and core; stand upright in a 9-inch square baking pan. To make filling, combine granola, dates, walnuts, cinnamon, nutmeg, lemon juice, and 3 tablespoons of the honey. Spoon equal amounts of filling into center of each apple (pack filling in lightly). Combine the remaining honey with butter and apple juice; pour over apples.

Cover and bake in a 350° oven for 30 minutes. Remove cover and bake, basting with pan juices several times, until apples are tender when pierced (about 35 minutes longer). Serve warm or cooled. At the table, pass a pitcher of cream to pour over each apple. Makes 6 servings.

Per serving (including cream): 3 grams protein, 49 grams carbohydrate, 35 milligrams cholesterol, 316 calories.

Brandied Ricotta with Fruit

For elegance with ease, this dessert reigns supreme. You just beat ricotta cheese with flavorings and sugar, chill, then surround with cookies and fruit slices. Your guests spread the cheese mixture on their choice of fruit and cookies, or make their own open-faced cooky sandwiches.

- **1 pint (2 cups) ricotta cheese**
- **¼ cup powdered sugar**
- **2 tablespoons brandy**
- **¼ teaspoon ground cinnamon**
- **8 plums or small peaches or 2 dozen unhulled whole large strawberries**
- **2 dozen mildly sweet cookies, such as petit beurre**

(Continued on next page)

With an electric mixer, beat together ricotta, powdered sugar, brandy, and cinnamon until smooth. Mound cheese mixture on a serving plate and swirl in a cone shape; cover lightly and chill for several hours.

To serve, surround with halved plums, small peach halves, or strawberries and accompany with cookies. To eat, spread on fruit and cookies. Makes 8 servings.

Per serving (including fruit and cookies): 8 grams protein, 26 grams carbohydrate, 31 milligrams cholesterol, 215 calories.

Sherried Cream with Fruit

This no-fuss dessert is elegant enough to serve your best company. You make a creamy pudding flavored with sherry, then layer it with fresh fruit in stemmed glasses.

- ⅓ **cup sugar**
- 2 **tablespoons cornstarch**
- ⅛ **teaspoon salt**
- 2 **cups milk**
- ¼ **cup cream sherry or apple juice**
- 2 **egg yolks, lightly beaten**
- 2 **tablespoons butter or margarine**
- 1 **teaspoon vanilla**
  About 1½ cups seedless red or green grapes, diced fresh pineapple, or sliced nectarines

In a 2-quart pan, stir together sugar, cornstarch, and salt. Gradually add milk and sherry until well blended. Set mixture over medium heat and cook, stirring constantly, until it boils; boil for 1 minute. Remove from heat.

Stir part of the hot sauce into beaten yolks, then return all to pan and cook for 30 seconds. Remove from heat and stir in butter and vanilla until butter is melted.

Layer spoonfuls of pudding and fruit in 4 stemmed glasses. If you use nectarines, be sure you end top layer with pudding so fruit will not darken. Chill until ready to serve. Makes 4 servings.

Per serving: 6 grams protein, 38 grams carbohydrate, 161 milligrams cholesterol, 285 calories.

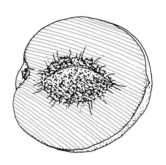

Fresh Berry Ice

This refreshing fruit ice is lighter than ice cream, cooler than sherbet, and packed with fresh fruit flavor. Best of all, with a tray of frozen fruit purée cubes ready in the freezer, you can whip up this low calorie dessert in minutes to serve one person or four.

It is best to make the ice into slush with a food processor. We give directions for using an electric mixer too, though the end result may be coarser and softer, and you may need to freeze the slush until it firms up.

- 3 **cups boysenberries, blackberries or olallieberries**
- ¾ **cup *each* water and sugar**
- 3 **tablespoons lemon juice**

In a blender or food processor, whirl berries until puréed. Pour through a sieve to remove seeds. Combine purée with water, sugar, and lemon juice. Mix well so sugar is dissolved. Freeze purée in divided ice cube trays. When purée is frozen, transfer cubes to plastic bags if you wish; return to freezer.

To serve, remove desired number of frozen purée cubes from

freezer and let stand for about 5 minutes at room temperature. With a food processor, whirl about 4 to 6 cubes at a time, using on-off bursts to break up the ice. Then process continuously until velvety. Spoon into serving containers and serve at once.

If you don't have a food processor, place ice cubes in a mixing bowl and smash them into small pieces with a wooden spoon. Then beat with an electric mixer until smooth—slowly at first, then gradually increasing to higher speeds. Beat purée into slush. Serve immediately. If texture is too soft, spoon into serving containers, then store in freezer until slush attains desired firmness. Makes 4 servings.

Per serving: 1.4 grams protein, 50 grams carbohydrate, no cholesterol, 203 calories.

Frozen Fruit Yogurts

Here's great party fun! Bring out the ice cream freezer and let everyone take a turn cranking out fruit-flavored frozen yogurt.

- **Sweetened fruit mixture (suggestions follow)**
- 3 **eggs, separated**
- ¼ **teaspoon *each* salt and cream of tartar**
- ¼ **cup sugar**
- 2 **quarts plain yogurt**

From the suggestions below, select the sweetened fruit mixture of your choice. Combine the suggested amounts of fruit, sugar, and honey (if used) in a 3-quart pan and bring to a boil, stirring, over high heat. Reduce heat to medium and cook, stirring constantly, until fruit softens and partially disintegrates (1 to 4 minutes). Remove from heat; stir in fruit juices, spices, and flavorings.

In a small bowl, lightly beat egg

yolks; stir in about ½ cup of the hot fruit mixture. Then stir yolk mixture into fruit mixture; cool to room temperature.

In a large mixing bowl, beat egg whites until frothy; add salt and cream of tartar and beat until soft peaks form. Gradually add the ¼ cup sugar and continue beating until stiff peaks form.

Turn yogurt into a 5-quart or larger bowl; fold fruit mixture into yogurt until well blended. Then gently fold yogurt-fruit mixture into egg whites. At this point, you can cover and refrigerate for several hours. When ready to process, transfer to a gallon-size or larger, hand-crank or electric ice cream freezer.

Assemble freezer according to manufacturer's directions, using about 4 parts ice to 1 part rock salt. When hand-cranking becomes difficult or electric motor stalls, remove the dasher. Once the yogurt has been turned and frozen, you can store the metal container in the freezer compartment of your refrigerator until serving time. Makes 1 gallon.

Apricot-orange. Use 4 cups thinly sliced unpeeled ripe **apricots,** 2 cups **sugar,** 2 tablespoons **lemon juice,** ½ cup **orange juice,** 1 teaspoon grated **orange peel,** and 4 teaspoons **vanilla.**

Per cup frozen apricot-orange yogurt: 5.5 grams protein, 40 grams carbohydrate, 56 milligrams cholesterol, 203 calories.

Banana-honey. Measure 4 cups thinly sliced ripe **bananas,** then coarsely mash them. Also use 1¼ cups **sugar,** ¾ cup **honey,** 3 tablespoons **lemon juice,** and 2 tablespoons **vanilla.**

Per cup frozen banana-honey yogurt: 5.5 grams protein, 46 grams carbohydrate, 56 milligrams cholesterol, 224 calories.

Peach. Use 4 cups sliced peeled **peaches,** 2 cups firmly packed **brown sugar,** 3 tablespoons **vanilla,** and ¾ teaspoon *each* **ground nutmeg** and **cinnamon.**

Per cup frozen peach yogurt: 5 grams protein, 40 grams carbohydrate, 56 milligrams cholesterol, 202 calories.

Raspberry. Use 4 cups lightly packed fresh (or unsweetened frozen and thawed) **raspberries,** 2 cups **sugar,** and 4 teaspoons *each* **lemon juice** and **vanilla.**

Per cup frozen raspberry yogurt: 5.5 grams protein, 38 grams carbohydrate, 56 milligrams cholesterol, 198 calories.

Broiled Pineapple & Bananas

Served hot with sour cream, this dish of glazed bananas is a delicious winter dessert to serve when other fresh fruit is scarce.

> 3 ripe bananas
> 6 slices fresh or canned pineapple
> ⅓ cup firmly packed brown sugar
> 2 tablespoons butter or margarine
> 1 tablespoon lemon juice
> ½ cup sour cream

Peel each banana and cut in half lengthwise, then crosswise, to make 4 pieces. You will have 12 pieces in all, 2 for each serving.

Arrange banana and pineapple in a single layer in a baking dish. Sprinkle brown sugar over the top, dot with butter, and sprinkle with lemon juice. Broil about 8 inches from heat, basting several times, until fruit is glazed (5 to 7 minutes). While still hot, arrange 2 pieces of banana and 1 piece of pineapple in each of 6 dessert dishes. Top each with a dollop of sour cream and spoon some of the hot butter sauce over the sour cream. Makes 6 servings.

Per serving: 1.5 grams protein, 37 grams carbohydrate, 20 milligrams cholesterol, 214 calories.

Strawberry Sundae

Fresh strawberries take three different shapes in this dessert— puréed for sauce, sliced to top the ice cream, and whole for garnish.

> 6 cups whole strawberries
> About ½ cup sugar
> 2 tablespoons orange-flavored liqueur (optional)
> ½ cup whipping cream
> 1 tablespoon sugar
> 3 cups strawberry ice cream

In a blender or food processor, whirl about 1½ cups of the strawberries until puréed; you should have 1 cup purée. Pour through a sieve to remove seeds. Stir ¼ cup of the sugar, along with liqueur (if used) into purée and mix well; cover and chill.

Set aside 8 whole berries for garnish. Slice remaining berries and sweeten with remaining ¼ cup sugar; cover and chill.

Just before serving, whip cream until thick. Sweeten with the 1 tablespoon sugar.

For each serving, place a scoop of ice cream in a small dessert bowl or goblet. Spoon about ½ cup sliced strawberries over ice cream and drizzle with about 2 tablespoons chilled strawberry sauce. Top with a dollop of whipped cream and a whole strawberry. Makes 8 servings.

Per serving (including liqueur): 3 grams protein, 33 grams carbohydrate, 36 milligrams cholesterol, 231 calories.

Cantaloupe Melba

Raspberry sherbet in goblets lined with sliced cantaloupe and topped with Melba sauce would make a memorable finale for a menu featuring an egg and cheese dish.

(Continued on next page)

2 cups fresh raspberries or unsweetened frozen raspberries, defrosted

⅓ cup sugar

2 tablespoons orange-flavored liqueur or raspberry-flavored brandy (optional)

2 small cantaloupes

3 cups raspberry sherbet

In a blender or food processor, whirl raspberries until puréed. Pour through a sieve to remove seeds. Stir sugar and liqueur (if used) into purée and mix well; cover and chill.

Halve cantaloupes and remove seeds; peel and cut into thin slices. Line each of 8 small dessert bowls or goblets with 3 or 4 melon slices. Top melon with a scoop of sherbet and pour 2 tablespoons chilled raspberry sauce over sherbet. Makes 8 servings.

Per serving (including liqueur): 2 grams protein, 45 grams carbohydrate, no cholesterol, 186 calories.

Half-cup Cookies

These crunchy drop cookies are nutritious enough for an on-the-go breakfast when coupled with a glass of milk.

2 cups whole wheat flour

1 teaspoon baking powder

¾ teaspoon salt

1 teaspoon ground cinnamon

2 eggs

¼ cup milk

½ teaspoon vanilla

½ cup *each* peanut butter, honey, and lightly packed brown sugar

½ cup (¼ lb.) butter or margarine, softened

½ cup semisweet chocolate or carob baking chips

½ cup chopped cashews, toasted almonds, or walnuts

½ cup *each* flaked coconut, raisins, and granola-type cereal

Combine whole wheat flour, baking powder, salt, and cinnamon; set aside.

In a large bowl, place eggs, milk, and vanilla; beat with an electric mixer. Beat in peanut butter, honey, brown sugar, and butter until creamy.

Stir in flour mixture until blended, then stir in chocolate chips, nuts, coconut, raisins, and granola until blended.

Drop batter, 1 heaping teaspoon at a time, about 1 inch apart on lightly greased baking sheets. Bake in a 375° oven for about 10 minutes or until cookies are golden on the bottom. Cool on rack. Makes 5 dozen cookies.

Per cooky: 2 grams protein, 10 grams carbohydrate, 13 milligrams cholesterol, 87 calories.

Freezer Date Cookies

There's no sugar added—dates and coconut give these cookies natural sweetness, and walnuts add crunch.

½ cup (¼ lb.) butter or margarine, softened

1 egg

2 teaspoons vanilla

1 cup all-purpose flour

1 teaspoon baking powder

¼ teaspoon salt

1 cup *each* chopped pitted dates, shredded coconut, and chopped walnuts

With an electric mixer, beat butter with egg and vanilla until smooth. In a separate bowl, combine flour, baking powder, and salt. Gradually add flour mixture to creamed mixture; beat until blended. Stir in dates, coconut, and walnuts.

Form dough into two 1½-inch rolls and wrap in wax paper or foil; chill in freezer until firm enough to slice easily (about 2 hours) or for as long as 1 month.

With a sharp knife, cut rolls into ⅜-inch-thick slices. Place slices on a lightly greased cooky sheet and bake in a 350° oven for about 12 minutes or until golden. Cool on rack. Makes 5 dozen cookies.

Per cooky: 1 gram protein, 5 grams carbohydrate, 9 milligrams cholesterol, 53 calories.

Chewy Bran Bars

These are no-bake cookies made with peanut butter, raisins, and whole bran cereal. They're perfect after-school treats or breakfast take-alongs for hurried mornings.

2 tablespoons butter or margarine

¼ cup *each* peanut butter and firmly packed brown sugar

½ cup honey

1½ cups chopped walnuts

2 teaspoons ground cinnamon

1 teaspoon vanilla

⅛ teaspoon salt

½ cup raisins or chopped pitted prunes or dates

2 cups whole bran cereal

In a heavy 3-quart pan, combine butter, peanut butter, brown sugar, and honey. Cook over low heat, stirring constantly, just until mixture begins to boil. Remove from heat. Add walnuts, cinnamon, vanilla, and salt; stir until blended. Stir in raisins and bran cereal and mix until well coated.

Turn mixture into a well buttered 8 or 9-inch square pan.

With a buttered spatula, firmly press mixture into an even layer. Let cool until mixture begins to firm up (about 5 minutes). Cut into bars and let cool thoroughly. Store airtight at room temperature. Makes 16 bars.

Per bar: 4 grams protein, 24 grams carbohydrate, 4 milligrams cholesterol, 185 calories.

Index

Metric Conversion Table

To change	To	Multiply by
ounces (oz.)	grams (g)	28
pounds (lbs.)	kilograms (kg)	0.45
teaspoons	milliliters (ml)	5
tablespoons	milliliters (ml)	15
fluid ounces (fl. oz.)	milliliters (ml)	30
cups	liters (l)	0.24
pints (pt.)	liters (l)	0.47
quarts (qt.)	liters (l)	0.95
gallons (gal.)	liters (l)	3.8
Fahrenheit temperature (° F)	Celsius temperature (° C)	5/9 after subtracting 32